Thomas Bailey Saunders

The Quest of Faith

Being Notes on the Current Philosophy of Religion

Thomas Bailey Saunders

The Quest of Faith
Being Notes on the Current Philosophy of Religion

ISBN/EAN: 9783337069896

Printed in Europe, USA, Canada, Australia, Japan

Cover: Foto ©Lupo / pixelio.de

More available books at **www.hansebooks.com**

THE
QUEST OF FAITH

BEING

NOTES ON THE CURRENT PHILOSOPHY

OF RELIGION

*La Nature confond les pyrrhoniens, et la
Raison confond les dogmatiques.*
PASCAL.

BY

THOMAS BAILEY SAUNDERS

LONDON

ADAM AND CHARLES BLACK

1899

CONTENTS

CHAPTER I

PRELIMINARY . . . . . PAGE 1

CHAPTER II

AGNOSTICISM 10

CHAPTER III

THE SCEPTICAL ARGUMENT . . . 43

CHAPTER IV

A GIFFORD LECTURER 77

CHAPTER V

TELEOLOGY 101

CHAPTER VI

BUTLER ONCE MORE . . 134

CHAPTER VII

ROMAN CATHOLIC WRITERS 149

CHAPTER VIII

THE WITNESS OF HISTORY 174

THE QUEST OF FAITH

CHAPTER I

PRELIMINARY

THE essays here offered to the reader deal in the main with the question of religious belief. They deal only with such aspects of it as have lately attracted notice; and this is a restriction attended, I venture to think, with some advantage. Except in the shape which from time to time is most obvious and definite, the question, for all but special students, has little vitality. Moreover, unless some limit of the kind be imposed, the treatment of it is apt to become a mere academic exercise. If the objection be raised that any discussion which is confined to certain aspects of a subject must needs be fragmentary and inconclusive, I submit that on so vast a theme as Religion no inquiry can well be final or exhaustive, and that here at least I make small claim to any positive result. There is the humble task of surveying a portion of the ground, and, as far as may be, of tracing indications, with which, if it is at all successfully accomplished, I shall be well satisfied.

The extent to which the leaders of English opinion have recently pronounced upon this question in public is surely one of the more remarkable characteristics of our time. That the chiefs of our political parties, as well as some of the most eminent of our scientific teachers, have busied themselves with speculations that might be thought to constitute the exclusive domain of philosophers and theologians is a fact, the significance of which is not yet, perhaps, commonly recognised. Nor would it, I imagine, be easy to discover in the history of the modern world, even at a period when the burden of work was less formidable than now, another example of so many men occupied in the control of public affairs who were also applying their minds to the fundamental problems of religion. Certainly at the present moment any counterpart to this feature of our national life would be sought in the rest of Europe in vain. Although here we may have only an instance of that singular connection between politics and letters which has marked our annals, and which, far from diminishing with the progress of democratic and imperial ideas, seems to grow and flourish the more, there is something entirely new and noteworthy in the circumstance that contemporary statesmen like the late Mr. Gladstone, Lord Salisbury, Mr. Arthur Balfour, and the Duke of Argyll, greatly differing from one another in many respects, should all alike have exercised their literary powers in the discussion of matters so remote from the business of politics. While the intrinsic value of their contributions to the ultimate questions of religion, philosophy, and science will be variously assessed, few will hesitate to believe that authors of such prominence in the public eye must exercise a large influence on the formation of opinion. The quality of their influence, no less than the temper in which their work is approached, must also, of course, be much affected by their high position; and no one whose lot it has been to attempt some estimate of their writings will be likely to underrate the difficulty of freeing his judgment in such a case from all extraneous considerations. Here I ought to mention that I have had the honour of making the attempt, from time to time, in the columns of the *Athenæum*, and that to the proprietor of that journal my best acknowledgments are due for permission to use such portions of what I there wrote as may be incorporated with the following pages.

Possibly it may be said that the prevailing aspects of the question of religious belief are ephemeral, and that therefore it is hardly worth while to deal with them as though they were possessed of any permanent value. Ephemeral, in a sense, they doubtless are. The next generation may be plied with arguments as unlike those which obtain now, as the latter in their turn differ from the common arguments of forty years ago. But the inference sought to be drawn from the fact, if fact it be, is unwarranted. In the first place, arguments, superficially dissimilar, may be nearly or entirely identical in their significance, as is often the case with those of the profoundest character. In the second place, arguments may be transitory and yet not without their use. The history of religious speculation is strewn with dead theories which in their day satisfied a need and served a purpose. They sprang into life, flourished, decayed, and were forgotten. When they passed away, it was either because, being merely novel, their attraction was exhausted, or because they were refuted or no longer felt to be adequate. But as long as they prevailed, they helped to supply, in some sort, an embodiment of the problem to be solved. It is the same with the arguments and theories that flourish now. While some of them are old and possibly imperishable, the shape in which they appear to-day may not endure. Others may be destined to lose their force altogether. But whether it is the arguments themselves, or their existing shapes, that are ephemeral, they form, so long as they are alive, the only channel by which the question readily comes home to us.

By religious belief I do not mean any particular species of theological creed. With the exception of one chapter, what follows is not directly, or hardly even indirectly, concerned with systems and dogmas; although they, too, have exhibited in their time a great variety of phase, of which the latest is not the least remarkable. To show the extent to which certain doctrines have been modified or destroyed by recent achievements in science, history, and criticism, would be to tell a thrice-told tale. With that I am not concerned. For my present purpose the contents of a creed, so far as they are elaborations of a principle, or the filling out of a theory, are of secondary interest. All the religious beliefs, of whatever kind, likely to be entertained among those who may conceivably read these pages, rest in the end upon a general faith in the existence of a God. The fundamental question is whether and how far any such faith may be justified; and it is this question, in the shape which it now assumes, and in the language in which it is now discussed, that I venture to approach.

Even as compared with its treatment by the last generation, this question does not exhibit quite the same features or evoke the same arguments. If the claims of the traditional religion have been modified by the demands of science, we may also, I think, affirm that the demands of science have been modified by the objections of philosophy. We do not hear so much now of that combination of matter, force, and necessary law which in the days of Moleschott and Büchner was supposed by them and their adherents to explain all the phenomena of the universe. The very magnificence of the victories which science has achieved, and the use to which they have been put in the campaign against theology and philosophy, have directed fresh attention to the problems which underlie all science. That the existence of an independent material world is one of the presuppositions on which all investigation is based, and that science consists in further and further extending the materialistic and mechanical interpretation of nature, used, for example, to be commonplaces. From this to the assertion that science spells what is commonly called materialism—the doctrine, namely, that matter is the ultimate reality—is but a step; and it is a step which has often been taken. A generation ago Mr. Herbert Spencer only expressed the general view of most men of science when he said that, should the Idealist be right, Evolution is a dream; and we may, indeed, well argue that Evolution would have no meaning or application at all, if there were no material universe to be evolved. But many men of science now admit, and even proclaim, that, so far as their own analysis takes them, the reality which science investigates is phenomenal only—a state of consciousness—an idea. Materialism, as the final explanation, has been abandoned—nay, sometimes it has even been indignantly repudiated—by those who are best qualified to speak in the name of science. One of the most distinguished of them has declared, in unequivocal terms, that if he were forced to choose between Materialism and Idealism, he would elect for the latter. I offer no opinion here as to whether this statement of Mr. Huxley's can be reconciled with other statements in his writings; but it is at least evidence that the point of view adopted in Mr. Herbert Spencer's dictum, just quoted, does not to-day command the assent that was easily given when the words were first uttered.

Nor, again, is an attitude of blank denial in regard to religion so familiar a possibility now, perhaps, as used to be the case when the Darwinian hypothesis, in the vigour of its youth, was sweeping all before it. The atheist has been modified into an agnostic. That the new name represents a real difference of mental temper will, I think, be conceded. Some definite effects, too, may be traced to the change. Not only has it softened controversial manners; it has also varied the character of the dispute. By his plea on behalf of suspended judgment the agnostic has produced a result which at first he can hardly have anticipated. His doubts as to the possibility of knowledge in the province of religion have raised doubts as to the nature of all knowledge, in whatever province. As we shall presently see, he has supplied the religious apologist with the argument from scepticism, and has thus put into his hands a weapon that has done good service in the past, and is now pointed afresh.

Once more: while the Darwinian hypothesis made an end of the teleological argument in the older and commoner form, another form has attained a prominence which forty years ago it did not possess. The older argument was never irreproachable, as Hume and others abundantly showed. But, with the multitude, the contention that the structure and arrangement observable in particular organisms is evidence of an intelligent artificer was regarded as an irrefragable proof for theism, until it was suggested that structure and arrangement are determined by the free play of natural conditions. This explanation seemed for the moment to banish teleology altogether. In reality it has only widened the range. It has driven the teleologist to regard Nature once more as a whole, and to seek the evidence of design in evolution itself. Are we, he now asks, to suppose that this vast universe, with all the order and beauty and interest which it presents, is the outcome of a fortuitous combination of primeval atoms, and utterly devoid of any meaning or purpose whatever? I need scarcely say that the question is only another phase of the ancient dispute between Democritus and Anaxagoras : Is it mechanism or intelligence that finally rules the world?

Of these and similar problems I propose, then, to treat; with the object of ascertaining how far the recent discussion of them is likely to render the quest of faith an easier or a more difficult enterprise. The readers to whom this book is submitted are those who take a general interest in such topics, and are alive to the direction and importance of current controversies in the sphere of religious belief. I make no pretension to write for specialists. As the discussion is of a philosophical character, it will, of course, be impossible, even if it were desirable, entirely to avoid the use of philosophical terms; but an endeavour will be made to employ them sparingly, and to translate them, as far as may be, into common language. And as Agnosticism is the state of mind that is perhaps most generally characteristic of the present day, I shall begin by asking attention to some of its arguments, as they are advanced by the writer who is often regarded as its chief exponent in this country.

CHAPTER II

AGNOSTICISM

I

IF Agnosticism be only the admission that our life is surrounded with mystery, of which many solutions have been offered that solve nothing, then all sensible men are Agnostics. What is more reasonable, it may be thought, than to say *I do not know* in regard to matters which in all ages have evoked an infinite variety of opinion. Although *I do not know* is sometimes, perhaps, a convenient euphemism for *I do not care*, we are here concerned with the man who, after reflection, not only professes ignorance, but also endeavours to show the causes to which his ignorance is due. His main contention is either that the human mind is, by its very nature, unfitted to deal with the questions raised, or that there is insufficient evidence to warrant any answer.

In our own day this attitude towards the problems involved in religion has found no more resolute champion than the late Mr. Huxley, and large numbers of men and women, among both the educated and the illiterate, have adopted it from him. To ascertain how far his Agnosticism was a valid and consistent attitude is, therefore, a task of some importance. But the task is one which cannot well be undertaken without first of all considering what it was that he achieved in science, and in what temper he approached the subject of religion. On this head, however, my remarks shall be brief as may be.

Of the general results of Mr. Huxley's activity there is probably no better or more concise account than that which he gave himself. At the close of the modest autobiography prefixed to the first volume of his collected essays[1] he passed a judgment on the scope, and to some extent on the character, of his work with which no competent or sober critic will find it necessary to disagree.

> I have [he said] subordinated any reasonable, or unreasonable, ambition for scientific fame which I may have permitted myself to entertain to other ends; to the popularisation of science; to the development and organisation of scientific education; to the endless series of battles and skirmishes over evolution; and to untiring opposition to that ecclesiastical spirit, that clericalism, which in England, as everywhere else, and to whatever denomination it may belong, is the deadly enemy of science.

To this may be added that in the course of his biological studies early in life he was engaged in important researches, and that he might with justice have taken some pride in their results. With

[1] *Collected Essays.* By T. H. Huxley, F.R.S. 9 vols.

especial satisfaction he might have mentioned, for instance, the share which he had in expounding the structural relations between man and the lower animals, as they are set forth in a volume on *Man's Place in Nature*. But if it was not his good fortune to make any great discovery or to inaugurate any new movement, he achieved distinction of another kind. He rendered the service without which great discoveries are apt to lose some of their value. More clearly and cogently than any other of Darwin's disciples he explained and defended the theory of evolution, as reinforced by the Darwinian hypothesis. In the face of the opposition and the criticism which the hypothesis evoked, this was not an enterprise lightly to be regarded or demanding abilities of a common order; and assuredly, of those who embarked on it, no one acquitted himself with more zeal and energy, or was rewarded with a larger measure of success.

The exposition of a new hypothesis was, however, only a part, though a very essential part, of the work which was laid upon its adherents a generation ago. There were included in its range many branches of inquiry besides biology. It became, in a very real sense, a *novum organon*, a principle of vast application; and, as every one knows, the interest which the new hypothesis excited greatly strengthened and extended the claims of natural science in the scheme of human knowledge. To attempt a complete philosophical system on this fresh basis was a task which fell to another writer, but it was Mr. Huxley more than any other Englishman of his time who made the basis commonly intelligible. It was he who most effectively educated his countrymen, not alone in the bearings of this particular account of the origin of species, but also in the general applications of the new doctrine. The popularisation of science, or of serious knowledge of any kind, is a work which unsuccessful or idle persons are fond of disparaging. But he afforded the most complete proof that when it is undertaken with care and from the right motives, and carried out in the proper spirit, there is none of a more honourable character, and scarcely any of a greater utility. In his case, no doubt, the work of exposition was often made to serve a purpose that was not strictly relevant to the matter in hand. It requires no very extensive acquaintance with his essays to arrive at the conclusion that, while science is professedly their subject, they are often inspired by an anti-ecclesiastical temper, nor any very profound knowledge of the history of scientific discoveries to find an excuse for this temper in the fact that it is commonly the fate of such discoveries to be assailed with theological weapons. The particular system known to its enemies as clericalism, with all that the system comprises, was throughout his career the foe at which the writer habitually discharged the straightest and swiftest of his arrows. Nay, his exploits in thus exercising a considerable talent for sarcasm probably won him more popular attention than other and higher accomplishments.

That Mr. Huxley's adherence to the Darwinian hypothesis was in no wise mere advocacy is shown by a volume in which he marshalled a number of essays on Darwin and his work, written at various intervals, from the publication of the *Origin of Species* in 1859 to the appearance of an admirable obituary notice of its author contributed to the *Proceedings of the Royal Society* in 1888. If these essays display no lack of admiration for Darwin's achievements, it is a feeling that, in some degree, at least, has been shared by the civilised portion of mankind. But they display other features which are not so common, and which — in view of the scientific enthusiasm attending those achievements at the time — do credit no less to Mr. Huxley's sober temper and his critical insight than to his practical sagacity. That the theory of evolution was the right theory he never entertained any doubt. Of the evidence in its favour, that derived from the geological record alone would, as he contended, have been amply sufficient to support it. Some of this evidence is discussed at length in the volume of *Discourses Biological and Geological*, which forms a fitting complement to the *Darwiniana*. He there ventured so far as to affirm that if the theory had not existed, palæontologists would have been compelled to invent it, so clearly may the traces of evolution be seen in the study of the remains of Tertiary mammalia discovered since 1859. But on the further question as to the means by which evolution has been brought about, and as to the influence and effect of its several factors, he never professed to feel a like certainty.

Since present opinion on this question is in a state of something little short of chaos, and has found vent in discussions from which the personal element has not been altogether eliminated, it may be well to state once more that Mr. Huxley did not admit the Darwinian hypothesis to be anything more than an hypothesis. In 1860 he recorded his clear conviction that, as the evidence then stood, the case was not absolutely proven—that no group of animals having all the characters of a species had been shown to be originated by selection, whether artificial or natural. This, however, did not in his judgment detract from the value of Darwin's work as being "the most compendious statement of well-sifted facts bearing on the doctrine of evolution that had ever appeared." Again, eighteen years later he confessed that it was still doubtful how far natural selection suffices for the production of species; although he was then ready to maintain that, "if not the whole cause, it was at least a very important element in that operation." But he admitted with the utmost frankness that while evolution itself is "no longer an hypothesis, but an historical fact," the nature of the physiological factors to which it is due "is still open to discussion." That he was right when he declared in 1878 that the question was still undecided has since then been abundantly shown; and if he reprinted his observations without comment or qualification, it is tolerably fair evidence that he found nothing in the speculations of Mr. Wallace or Professor Weismann to induce him to alter his opinions.

In his treatment of the whole subject what is, perhaps, most remarkable is the manner in which he passed beyond the ground occupied by the hypothesis itself to its philosophical implications. He candidly avowed that he had little of the genuine naturalist in his mental composition, and that what he always cared for was the physiological question, "the architectural and engineering part of the business." But the study of general types is apt to lead to questions of still larger generality; and the essays on Darwin's work and on kindred topics form, indeed, relatively a small portion of those which he reprinted. Most of them were written with the object of expounding his views on religion and ethics, or of attacking the views of others. For in these larger questions he was, above all, a controversialist. His high competence in treating of matters wholly within the sphere of physical science was always admitted; but, as no one knew better than himself, he had to endure a large measure of the doubt which metaphysicians are in the habit of entertaining as to the truth and value of one another's conclusions.

II

Although in the popular estimate Mr. Huxley was commonly considered to be a philosopher of singular acumen, I confess that of his achievements in philosophy I find it difficult to speak with much admiration. If I venture to assert—what I take to be the truth—that he often pursued lines of criticism which cannot be reconciled one with another, I shall probably be met by the objection that many great writers are open to the same charge. That this is unhappily the case we are all of us aware. Inconsistency is the common lot. Nay, I should be sorry to maintain that the opposite quality is always a virtue, or that an eminent thinker was wrong when he described it as "the vice of little minds." But unquestionably a philosopher who is not at one with himself is to that extent unphilosophic ; and the less coherent the several aspects of a theory, the smaller is the claim which it can make to finality. Tried by this standard, Mr. Huxley's writings, vigorous though they be, and of an admirable lucidity of style, exhibit many shortcomings. Take his statements by themselves, and some of them possibly may appear to be well founded ; but compare them one with another, and contradictions of the most palpable kind ensue.

For example: as the result of certain physiological researches, which are described with rare skill and lucidity, he arrived at the conviction that man is a conscious automaton, and that consciousness, including volition, is only a concomitant of certain molecular changes in the brain.[1] As for the truth of this view, I am not here concerned either to affirm or to deny it. Possibly this theory of the relation between mind and matter may best explain the facts; but what I am concerned to point out is that the writer who held it elsewhere stated his belief, and stated it with great emphasis, that consciousness is neither matter nor force, nor any conceivable modification of either one or the other.[2] Further, he admitted, in a manner as uncompromising as the most ardent idealist could desire, that consciousness is the one ultimate certainty in the universe, and that the existence of matter is, at most, but "a highly probable hypothesis." Yet in spite of this he had no hesitation in declaring that "we have as much reason for regarding the mode of motion of the nervous system as the cause of the state of consciousness as we have for regarding any event as the cause of another." The mutual antagonism of these statements must be obvious to the most casual reader. If consciousness be the ultimate certainty, how can it conceivably be an effect of changes in that very matter which only exists for it as a probable hypothesis?

Again, if volition is only an indication of molecular change, and never a cause of it, what possi-

[1] I. *Animal Automatism*, 244.   [2] IX. *Science and Morals*, 130.

bility is there of reconciling this doctrine with the further statement that the conscious automaton is "endowed with free will in the only intelligible sense of that much-abused term; that is to say, that in many respects he can do as he likes." I doubt whether the proposition that a conscious automaton can in any respect do as he likes is one to which it is possible to attach any meaning whatever. Mr. Huxley, it is clear, was anxious to disown the title of fatalist. He did, indeed, disown it in so many words; but he gave a curious reason for so doing. "I take the conception of necessity," he said, "to have a logical and not a physical foundation." Now he defined "necessary" as that of which we cannot conceive the contrary.[1] But that of which we cannot conceive the contrary is not quite the same thing as that which is fated or certain to happen; for of this we may not only conceive, but often strongly desire, the contrary. To regard necessity as a logical conception does not, then, disprove that the writer who so regards it is a fatalist. Nor is it easy to apprehend how such a conscious automaton as has been described can in any intelligible sense be affected by moral reproof or exhortation, unless volition can in some way bring about molecular change; and yet many of the finest passages in these *Collected Essays* are charged with a moral purpose. If the working of an automaton cannot be modified by moral lessons, such lessons are useless; if it

[1] I. 193.

can, what we have to do with is not an automaton.

But the most serious contradiction of all is apparent when we come to examine the doctrine of Agnosticism. In the war of philosophical and theological opinion in which he found himself engaged, Mr. Huxley at a certain period of his career declared that he was unable to side with any party, or to adopt any of the names by which his contemporaries were content to describe their beliefs or the lack of them. It is well known that afterwards, perceiving the advantages of a label, he invented a word to express his intellectual position. With characteristic humour he described how he came to apply it to himself in the debates of a deceased philosophical society. But he complained more than once,—nor perhaps without cause,—that some of his antagonists had misrepresented the meaning which he attached to the word. He therefore defined it, not as a creed, but as a method. The essence of the method lay, he declared, in the rigorous application of a single principle as old as Socrates, stated afresh by Descartes, and prevailing to-day as "the fundamental axiom of modern science."

> Positively the principle may be expressed: In matters of the intellect, follow your reason as far as it will take you, without regard to any other consideration. And negatively: In matters of the intellect, do not pretend that conclusions are certain which are not demonstrated or demonstrable.[1]

---

[1] V. *Agnosticism*, 246.

Now, regarded simply as a definition, nothing might seem on the surface to be clearer or more direct than this statement. Nothing, it may be added, could be more unacceptable to the old orthodoxy or to any system based on a supernatural revelation. If with modern orthodoxy the fate of the principle might not be so sure, that is only because the foundations of modern orthodoxy are in the highest degree uncertain. But wherever the definition finds acceptance, its value will be allowed to depend on the meaning and the scope of its words. These are by no means so clear as they may seem. In the whole of our philosophical terminology there is, perhaps, no word that can be used in so many senses as "reason." It may signify mind in general, or a special faculty of mind, or the exercise of such a faculty. Again, reason may mean reasoning; and reasoning in its turn may cover processes that differ as widely as induction and the use of the syllogism. We may justly ask whether, in resolving to "follow your reason as far as it will take you," any distinction can be made between reason as the process of valid ratiocination, and reason as the inductive apprehension of ultimate ideas; whether in "matters of the intellect" any and every kind of knowledge is included; and, finally, what we mean or imply by "demonstration." Logicans agree, I believe, that in any strict sense of the word all demonstration either rests on undemonstrable axioms or definitions, or else somewhere begs the truth of the very proposition to be proved. The demonstrations given by Euclid ultimately rest on certain axioms and definitions assumed at the outset to be true; and the beginner in geometry is commonly told that for these axioms and definitions proof is not only not required, but is not possible. Similarly, in the familiar demonstration by syllogism that Socrates is mortal, because all men are mortal, and he is a man, it needs no great acumen to perceive that in premising that all men are mortal, the demonstrator included Socrates from the first, and thereby took his mortality for granted.

If there are any "ultimate ideas" which are of the first importance in the sphere of investigation to which Mr. Huxley devoted himself, they are the existence of an independent material world, the uniformity of nature, the credibility of our senses. Unless a material world is assumed to exist, unless its phenomena are conceived, under some aspect, as presenting invariable sequences commonly called "laws," and unless we believe that what our senses tell us is provisionally true, there can be no such thing as science. But the very character of these "ultimate ideas"—these presuppositions of all science—is that they are neither demonstrated nor demonstrable. They are pure assumptions, on which reason, in the sense in which the word is obviously employed in Mr. Huxley's definition, would act as a ready solvent. It is plain that any rigorous application of the Agnostic principle to these assumptions would lead to the conviction that there can be no ultimate certainty about anything. Something must be assumed before anything can be proved. When, therefore, Mr. Huxley declared that Agnosticism, as it is here defined, was "the fundamental axiom of modern science," he seems to have overlooked the fact that were it to be rigorously applied it would make an end of science altogether.

Nor elsewhere in his writings did Mr. Huxley appear to be unaware that this is the case. In an essay on *Possibilities and Impossibilities*[1] he argued that nothing has a right to the title of "an impossibility" except a contradiction in terms, and that we are not justified in any *à priori* assertion that the order which experience reveals to us cannot change. "Our highest and surest generalisations remain," he there declared, "on the level of justifiable expectations; that is, very high probabilities." He held it inconceivable that any intelligence like ours could possess grounds for certainty which would stand the test of strict logic. But in spite of these admissions, he claimed that we do possess a certainty of a kind which, if not logical, he was ready to call rational. In remarkable language he repudiated any desire to weaken the grounds on which this certainty rests. But what is this, strictly, but to give up the principle of Agnosticism as just defined? Nay, he was ready to confess, as he urged in another

[1] V. 192.

passage in the same essay, that it is by "an act of faith" that we take the experience of the past as our guide to the present and the future. His faith may not, indeed, have been of the sort which removes mountains, but it was sufficiently robust. "To quarrel," he said, "with the uncertainty which besets us in intellectual affairs would be about as unreasonable as to object to live one's life, with due thought for the morrow, because no man can be sure that he will be alive an hour hence." For my part, however, I would submit that if modern science or any scheme of organised knowledge were, as regards its "fundamental axioms," in a condition as unstable as that of human life, and had no better or more certain prospect, there would be hardly any call to devote our lives to it; and that, had we not the assurance that the higher flights of the mind reach to something fixed and permanent, our individual existence would have no stay or value.

What, then, is the conclusion to be drawn from these observations? It is, I take it, that Agnosticism cannot be a "fundamental axiom" of any branch of thought; that something may be true, rationally, certain, necessary — what you will — that is also undemonstrated and indemonstrable? and that if Mr. Huxley were an Agnostic at all, he was an inconsistent one. He knew as well as any man that science cannot build, and that its conclusions are worthless, except on the assumption of the uniformity of nature; and to cast doubt on that assumption, or to refuse to accept it because it cannot be demonstrated, is to weaken the foundation of science ; to show, in fact, that it rests upon sand. Unless uniformity be assumed, we are not justified in the assertion that the laws of nature, as we know them to-day, were in force a hundred years ago, or will remain so until next week ; or that an event which in modern times would be called a miracle may not have been a perfectly normal phenomenon in antiquity. Whatever opinion Mr. Huxley may have held as to the theoretical value of Agnosticism, he could not and did not in practice elevate the principle to the rank of an axiom, if the word be used in the sense attached to it by every metaphysician from Aristotle downwards, as that which is assumed as the basis of demonstration. More than once he quoted with approval Goethe's aphorism on *thätige Skepsis*,—on that active, practical, and efficacious scepticism which aims at conquering itself, and arriving through experience at conditioned certainty. Therefore clearly the Agnosticism which he advocated in dealing with religion is limited in its application, and in the strict sense of the word is a method only. We may best, perhaps, describe it as a mental habit—the habit of demanding and of appraising evidence for what it is worth. But the rigorous investigation of evidence leads to principles and axioms which cannot be questioned. So far is Agnosticism from being itself a principle that, ultimately, it cannot even be applied to principles. It is a method applicable only to the approaches to knowledge, but then always applicable — nay, indispensable. It is no more than the practice of free inquiry, which is honoured, not in the breach, but in the observance, and is the indisputable privilege of all honest men. To come to the bottom of the whole matter, unless Agnosticism is simply intellectual suicide in disguise, it must have knowledge, certain and assured, as its natural goal. In science, at least, this is a truth which Mr. Huxley always recognised.

His Agnosticism, indeed, would have little interest but for the application which he made of it to religion. The great question of the time, as he declared, is that of nature *versus* supernature. Of the latter he was wont to affirm that we know nothing. What we know and what we do not know, what is true and what is not true, are questions, of course, which must be determined by evidence; and here Agnosticism is a highly convenient word to express an attitude of reasoned ignorance respecting that of which we have no evidence, or of which the evidence is insufficient to lead us to any sure conclusion. The manner in which Mr. Huxley applied this principle to religion is well known. Adopting the *rôle* which he himself had attributed to some ecclesiastical Moses controlling scientific inquiry, he barred "an ancient and indefeasible right of way" into what is popularly called the supernatural. He set up a "comminatory noticeboard," advising all whom it may concern that here there was no thoroughfare. In plain language, he declared that an inquiry which has engaged the attention of some of the best and wisest of mankind in all ages is through lack of evidence to be proscribed altogether. But is there such a lack of evidence as he asserted? To those who desire to prosecute the inquiry, I shall venture to maintain that what he enclosed as supernatural should more properly be called supersensuous; nay, that under that name he himself roamed in it at will.

That we can know nothing of a supernature, if the term means something outside nature as "the totality of all which is," no reasonable man will deny. But if we investigate this totality, we must have equal regard to its two aspects of matter and mind. In regard to its aspect as matter we have reached a definite conclusion. We have discovered that in the field of physical science we must assume a foundation for our knowledge which is not susceptible of logical proof. In respect of the truth of this foundation we cannot be Agnostics, although it is a truth which cannot be demonstrated. Further, the certainty which we entertain, resting as it ultimately does on an assumption, is of a supersensuous character. Evidence for this certainty there doubtless is; but although pointing to ultimate principles, the evidence can never be of a kind to prove them. Now if axioms are necessary to a system of physical science, and the Agnostic can entertain no doubt as to their truth, although it be indemonstrable, may he not also be required to show cause why he should entertain any doubt as to the truth of the postulates necessary to other systems of thought? If, for example, we find on analysis that, whatever sceptical difficulties are attached to our conceptions of the existence of God, the freedom of the will, and immortality, the evidence of moral phenomena is such that a coherent theory of them must take some postulate involving these conceptions as its foundation, by what right would the Agnostic refuse to recognise this postulate as true, so long as he recognised ethics at all? We have, I apprehend, neither more nor less right to posit uniformity in the physical world than we have to posit, let us say, the absolute nature of duty in the ethical. It is true that ethical differs from physical theory in the matter with which it deals, and in so far as it implies obedience to an obligation; yet both have to deal with evidence, and the evidence in either case is not intelligible except on the basis of propositions which cannot be proved, but still are necessary.

In his essay on *Science and Morals*, Mr. Huxley made some attempt to deal with this subject of moral postulates. All that he found to say was that physical science had no objection to offer to them; but that if any one could tell him how he knew that they were true, it was just the man whom he wanted to see. The answer to this question is, that if they are untrue, there is no such thing as a moral law;

just as, if there is no uniformity in nature, there is no such thing as a physical law; and further, that as the naturalist arrives at his axiom by experience of nature, so the moralist discovers his postulate by experience of morality. As morality is something essentially practical, rational certainty as to the truth of its postulates can be attained only in practice; even as the physical philosopher attains his clear conviction that nature is uniform from familiarity with its phenomena.

This is, in fact, the method which great moralists have actually followed. We are all aware that Kant, while he showed that the existence of God, the freedom of the will, and immortality were ideas beyond the reach of pure reason, nevertheless recognised that practical reason afforded the assurance of their truth. He found himself compelled to accept them as postulates necessary to the moral consciousness, and involved in its fundamental and indemonstrable principle of a Categorical Imperative, or the command so to act as that our action may be fit for law universal. Goethe, too, for whom Mr. Huxley evinced so much admiration, was also of opinion, as he declared to Eckermann, that the existence of God is a postulate gained in the experience of practical life. Nor is it only the greatest philosophers and poets who have held this view. What, after all, is the difference between the conception of a moral postulate entertained by a Kant and a Goethe, and that which was presented long ago in the language of the Fourth Gospel: "If any man will do his will, he shall know of the doctrine."

There is a passage at the close of Mr. Huxley's *Life of Hume* which illustrates this argument in a remarkable manner, and shows us, I think, that in spite of all his Agnostic professions he was not so sure of his ground as he fancied himself to be.

> In whichever way [he said] we look at the matter, morality is based on feeling, not on reason; though reason alone is competent to trace out the effects of our actions, and thereby dictate conduct. Justice is founded on the love of one's neighbour; and goodness is a kind of beauty. The moral law, like the laws of physical nature, rests in the long run upon instinctive intuitions, and is neither more nor less "innate" and "necessary" than they are.

It is plain that the truth of instinctive intuitions does not admit of being demonstrated. According to the words which I have quoted, the foundation of the moral law is a conception that is valid, though indemonstrable. How ill this harmonises with the Agnostic principle, in any rigorous application of it, the reader will perceive for himself.

Further, as in science and art we take our ultimate conceptions from the teaching of those who possess an innate faculty for these branches of knowledge, "the Pascals and Mozarts, Newtons and Raffaelles," so, said Mr. Huxley, there are "men of moral genius, to whom we owe ideals of duty and visions of moral perfection which ordinary mankind could never have attained." In the same way, he would not, I take it, have denied that we owe our ultimate conceptions of religion to men of religious genius; or that religion is any more or any less of a human invention than literature, science, or art. They are all of them, I venture to assert, alike mysteries, at which the common man could never have arrived of himself. But if this be so; if in other matters we learn our lesson from men of splendid gifts, why, in matters of the moral and religious consciousness, should we refuse a similar guidance? Why should we accept ultimate conceptions at the hands of the masters of science and art, and refuse them at the hands of the masters of religion and morality? By what dialectical legerdemain are we to hold the Agnostic method in abeyance in the one case, and enforce it in the other?

III

If any further evidence be needed to prove that Mr. Huxley's views on the subject of morality are hardly to be reconciled with his scientific doctrines, that evidence exists in abundance in his lecture on *Evolution and Ethics.* Delivered to the University of Oxford, the lecture was in many ways a remarkable performance, whether it be regarded merely as a literary achievement, or as the channel of surprising views. There, more than in any other of his writings or speeches, Mr. Huxley left himself free to treat a wide subject in a wide spirit, untrammelled by the influence of special studies. There, as elsewhere, it was an advantage to him that, in spite of strong scientific interests, and the limits which they often impose upon minds imbued with them, he possessed a natural liking for the atmosphere of general culture, of which we may reasonably presume that, if a man can breathe it without intoxication, it is likely to inspire him with the clearest observations and the soundest conclusions. Whatever opinion may be formed as to the accuracy of Mr. Huxley's observations or the value of his conclusions, there can be no doubt as to the wide range of his view, or the solid character of his acquaintance with modes of thought which have no patent connection with modern scientific doctrines.

No less remarkable than the range of his view was the dexterous manner in which the prophet of Agnosticism contrived to lecture before a professedly Christian University and enforce a doctrine that in its essential character was an approximation to the Pauline dogma of nature and grace, without making a single direct reference to the tenets of Christendom. For the lecture was, in truth, an attempt to show how the Pauline dogma answers to the needs of human life in its conflict with the workings of nature, and closely accords with scientific principles. Mr. Huxley sought to effect this demonstration by the following argument: As civilisation gradually tempers the savagery of nature, the advantages of life in society become, he urged, so apparent that men were forced to reflect upon them. The ethical sense largely arose in and from the conception of justice involved in the very idea of society. Justice was found, in fact, to be a necessary element in social existence. But the sense or conviction that "society is impossible unless those who are associated agree to observe certain rules of conduct towards one another," soon came to distinguish between a guilty action and a merely wrong one. Justice began to appreciate the bearings of motive on the quality of the act, and thus led to the further conception of desert. "Righteousness, that is, action from right motive, not only became synonymous with justice, but the positive constituent of innocence and the very heart of goodness." Observers of life found, however, that, as a matter of fact, its pains and pleasures were by no means distributed according to desert, and that the nature of things was radically unjust. Hence the tragedy of life; hence the conclusion that "cosmic nature is no school of virtue, but the headquarters of the enemy of ethical nature." Now if, as no one can doubt, both good and evil may be either increased or diminished by human action, it is the paramount duty of ethical man to seek to diminish the pain and suffering that come in the train of the cosmic process, and, in fact, to combat that process at every step. This conclusion Mr. Huxley stated in the plainest language:—

> The practice of that which is ethically best—what we call goodness or virtue—involves a course of conduct which, in all respects, is opposed to that which leads to success in the cosmic struggle for existence.

When we remember that the man who uttered these words had spent the burden and the heat of his day in promulgating the theory of evolution by means of natural selection, while his scientific friends and followers were labouring to show that that theory afforded a satisfactory explanation of all manner of problems, psychological, ethical, and religious, so uncompromising a pronouncement in favour of grace as something opposed to nature is undoubtedly of great interest.

In estimating the value of this lecture it is important to observe, in the first place, that the sum and substance of the lecturer's remarks is a vigorous denunciation of what he called "the fanatical individualism of our time." The system of which he gave this uncomplimentary description is an attempt, made by certain philosophers, who need not be named, to apply the analogy of cosmic nature to society. They argue that inasmuch as certain forces have produced beneficent results in the one order, there is a fair presumption in favour of their producing equally beneficent results in the other, if only these forces are left to themselves. But it is not difficult to destroy this argument by insisting upon the artificial character of civilisation, which creates and vindicates its own code of conduct; just as, to go a step further, it is in a great measure by protesting against the artificial character of civilisation that the doctrines of individualistic naturalism gain any acceptance. Mr. Huxley maintained that we should frankly recognise morality as something unnatural, in the sense that the ethical process is not only distinct from, but entirely inimical to, the cosmic process. He supported his contention by dwelling upon the fallacy of supposing that what is fittest in nature is necessarily best in ethics, and upon the indubitable fact that the cosmic process gives as much sanction to immoral as to moral sentiments. "The history of civilisation," he said, "details the steps by which men have succeeded in building up an artificial world within the cosmos"; and as civilisation has everywhere advanced and worked beneficially by the interference of man with nature, so the ethical process is an interference of a similar character, from which as much may be hoped in the way of improvement.

When he denounced the view that justice is merely the ethical aspect of a biological law tending to the survival of the fittest, Mr. Huxley assumed a position which was no less interesting than valuable. The general sentiment of mankind in all ages is against the adoption of any such opinion as was laid down, for instance, by Mr. Herbert Spencer in his work on *Justice*. It was there asserted that ethical action is that which "favours the maintenance of the individual and the preservation of the race"; with the corollary that acts are right or wrong according as they tend or do not tend to the continuance of the species. There can be no doubt that one aspect of the ethical process is described with entire accuracy in the theory which Mr. Huxley advanced. It would be folly to deny that in particular cases the ethical man has often to oppose the natural man. But to make this opposition the distinguishing characteristic of morality is a very different matter. That the ethical man must always oppose the natural man, or that ethics and nature are in any radical and permanent enmity, is a proposition attended by a great many difficulties, and in the mouth of an exponent of evolution a particularly hard saying.

Although we can hardly expect that every side of the relation between the natural and the ethical process could be examined in a discourse extending only to thirty or forty pages, there is one point involved in the theory advanced by Mr. Huxley which, I venture to say without fear of contradiction, was insufficiently considered; although it is very essential not only to any acceptance, but even to any right understanding of that theory. The point, perhaps, may best be put by asking the question whether this ethical process, which is regarded as altogether opposed to the cosmic process, is or is not a part of the cosmic process; and if it is not so opposed, what account can be given of its origin? How are we to maintain, or in what way can we even conceive, that anything can arise within the cosmic process which, in the lecturer's comprehensive phrase, "is in all respects opposed" to the working of that process?

To this question Mr. Huxley did not directly address himself in the course of his remarks, although he did, indeed, refer to "a fund of energy" lying in man, "operating intelligently, and so far akin to that which pervades the universe, that it is competent to influence and modify the cosmic process." But in one of the notes appended to the lecture, and again and more at length in certain "prolegomena" afterwards prefixed to it, Mr. Huxley raised this all-important question, and gave an answer which shows that he was by no means unaware of the difficulty. The answer, however, is hard to reconcile with the theory, and suggests, indeed, an important modification of it.

> Of course [he said], strictly speaking, social life and the ethical process, in virtue of which it advances towards perfection, are part and parcel of the general process of evolution, just as the gregarious habit of innumerable plants and animals, which has been of immense advantage to them, is so. . . . The tendency of individuals to over self-assertion is kept down by fighting. Even in these rudimentary forms of society, love and fear come into play, and enforce a greater or less renunciation of self-will. To this extent the general cosmic process begins to be checked by a rudimentary ethical process, which is, strictly speaking, part of the former, just as the "governor" in a steam engine is part of the mechanism of the engine.

Now the application of this note is, I think, obvious. If in rudimentary forms of society the use of the "governor" is only to modify the working of the machine, why in highly-developed forms of society should it be the aim of the "governor" to oppose the machine altogether? The business of this necessary device is only to modify the working of the machine so that it shall give the best results. Nor is it otherwise, I submit, with the state of grace in its relation to the state of nature. Were the ethical process described as an agency which directs and controls rather than entirely opposes the cosmic process, there would be little in the theory to criticise. But, as I happen to know from somewhat frequent conversation with him, Mr. Huxley was unwilling to accept control or modification as a substitute for the opposition which he affirmed to exist.

An objection of a different but still more fatal character may be taken to the solution of the difficulty which he supplied in his "prolegomena." Speaking of the ethical process as born of the cosmic process, and yet in essential antagonism with it, he maintained that the distinction which he sought to establish between the two was of the same justifiable and useful kind as that between "works of art" and "works of nature," where it is obvious that both are products of the cosmic process. Even in a state of nature what, he asked, is the struggle for existence but the antagonism of the results of the cosmic process in the region of life, one to another? Nay, he endeavoured to put the case still more simply :—

When a man lays hold of the two ends of a piece of string and pulls them, with intent to break it, the right arm is certainly exerted in antagonism to the left arm; yet both arms derive their energy from the same original source.

Had the ethical process, as I say, been held to be a part of the cosmic process which regulated or controlled other parts of it, the illustration would undoubtedly hold good. But Mr. Huxley used language which can only mean that he regarded the opposition between the cosmic and the ethical process as radical and complete. If in this illustration the man stands for the cosmic process, and his arms for the "state of nature" and the "state of art" respectively, it is clear that, although the arms are in antagonism with each other, one of them cannot conceivably be regarded as acting in antagonism with the man himself. Yet if the analogy is to hold, such is the proposition which we should be required to accept. The conclusion which the plain man will not, I think, fail to reach is that if morality is to be defined as being in *essential* antagonism with the cosmic process, morality cannot conceivably be a product of it, or derive its energy from the same source.

Some other considerations may be mentioned which make against Mr. Huxley's theory. A strict application of it would appear to involve the assumption that nature in itself is wholly and necessarily an evil, at any rate from the point of view of ethical man; whereas Mr. Huxley was most careful to insist that the cosmic process has no sort of relation to moral ends. If that be so, it is difficult to understand how the essence of morality can consist in opposing what is non-moral. As against any essential opposition between nature and morality, it may be urged that there are many tendencies of the cosmic process which morality approves. Sometimes when nature revenges itself on those who break its laws, morality contemplates the revenge with satisfaction. Further, to attain its ends, the ethical process often makes use of the methods of the cosmic process. Mr. Huxley referred to the methods of the ape and the tiger as highly characteristic of the cosmic process. We will say nothing of the methods of the ape; but society uses the methods of the tiger against those of its members who offend its laws. That is to say, society directs one of the chief agencies of the cosmic process into a channel in which its operation is useful to society; much as the miller uses the stream, which if left to itself might inundate his fields, to grind his corn. And the axe and the rope with which, as we are told, civilised man "does his best to put an end to the survival of the fittest of former days," what are they but methods of nature which society finds suited to its own development? Again, the history of civilisation reveals the fact that the canons of morality constantly shift and change in accordance with the circumstances in which society for the time finds itself. If, then, as seems to be the case, morality exists for man, and not man for morality, surely the moral man must at least aim at being in a state of harmony with himself, and not in a state of continuous self-repression. The wisest thinkers, ancient and modern, lay most stress on this positive element in morality, in virtue of which its action is directed not so much to the mortification of natural instincts as to the use of them for worthy ends. According to Plato, justice is a harmony of different parts of the soul; according to Goethe the highest state is one of tranquillity, in which a man "loves what he commands himself to do." There does not seem to be room for this conception of morality in any strict interpretation of the theory which Mr. Huxley defended.

The incongruity between the origin of morality, as described by some men of science, and the high character of the moral creed which they themselves profess, has often been noted. It would, I think, pass the wit of man to devise any explanation that will reconcile the ethical theory which Mr. Huxley adopted towards the close of his career with the scientific principles which he spent the greater part of his career in proclaiming. That his moral creed was sufficiently earnest is beyond doubt. We may disagree with his account of the relation between evolution and ethics; we may question the consistency of his Agnosticism, yet no one can fail to be moved by the eloquence of his plea on behalf of a noble life, even though he held out no hope that in the end nature will be overcome by grace.

> The theory of evolution [he said] encourages no millennial anticipations. If for millions of years our globe has taken the upward road, yet some time the summit will be reached and the downward route be commenced. The most daring imagination will hardly venture upon the suggestion that the power and intelligence of man can ever arrest the procession of the great year.

Nevertheless he suffered no reflection of this nature to weaken his argument (which in its force and ardour might have come from the most zealous transcendentalist) that morality is, in the last resort, justice and righteousness; and that the highest duty of ethical man is to combat the pain and suffering that are everywhere apparent in the world.

Mr. Huxley's theory may be right or it may be wrong. But if it be right, I, at least, fail to perceive how the Agnostic principle can have any bearing on morality. We have seen, in the course of this chapter, that that principle, applied to the foundations of science, would make science impossible. It is not applied to morality at all, but simply ignored. A principle which thus proves its incompetence in dealing with the most vital questions presented by the physical world and the social relations of human beings is scarcely in a position to claim acceptance, unsuspected and unchallenged, in the complex sphere of thought, feeling, and duty which we call religion.

CHAPTER III

THE SCEPTICAL ARGUMENT

I

I NOW proceed to examine some of the arguments that have been generally advanced in support of theistic belief. Of these one of the most important may be described as partly negative in its character. Theistic belief is urged upon us as the sole escape from the paralysis of sceptical despair. We are told that the existence of God is the only hypothesis which will supply us either with a sure foundation for knowledge, or with a proper standard for the guidance of life.

In our own day the argument has been presented in an attractive shape and with some novel accessories in Mr. Arthur Balfour's *Foundations of Belief*.[1] Whatever may be the value or the logical coherence of that work, there is no disputing the fact of its high significance. That when it first

[1] *The Foundations of Belief:* being Notes introductory to the Study of Theology. By the Right Hon. Arthur James Balfour.

appeared critics differed as to the service which it was to render to religion was inevitable. There were some who accepted it with a feeling of real enthusiasm, as though it had struck a fresh note. Others, again, more ardent than the rest, hastened to assert that it was about to form a turning-point in the history of theological controversy. The reader will scarcely need to be reminded that similar prophecies have often been made before, and almost as often have miscarried; or that the fate which attends on books gives no warrant to the supposition that those which are ushered in with a blare of trumpets are destined to exercise the most enduring influence. Mr. Balfour's work, although of undeniable distinction, does not, I make bold to say, contain any theories that are both new and true; in the realm of philosophy, indeed, such theories seem hardly any longer possible. But what can be affirmed with tolerable certainty is that no other work of recent publication has brought to its appointed task so much new force and emphasis, combined with the same likelihood of attracting widespread attention. It exhibits in a fashion that no one can mistake the growth of the revolt against the application of the general methods of natural science to philosophy and theology, and herein it embodies the salient features of contemporary thought. It does so with great vigour and effect. The public position of the author, not to mention the admiration for his abilities which is entertained by men of all parties, would of itself be sufficient to secure him a large hearing for any reasoned utterance on a question of broad human interest. As for the literary qualities of the work, there is scarcely any need to dwell upon them. No one who reads it can fail to be aware that the attention which the writer and the subject command is enhanced by the fascinating lucidity of the style, by its wit, its graceful irony, its dignity, and at times its great eloquence.

In laying his foundations so much of Mr. Balfour's work consists in clearing the ground that, without some acquaintance with the manner in which he undertakes this preliminary operation, no sufficient estimate of his positive argument can be formed. He declares at the outset that he writes for the general reader rather than for the specialist in philosophy, and that his object is to recommend a particular attitude towards the problems of the world. In order that his views may have the advantage of being exhibited against the background of some contrasted system of thought, he selects the only one that, as he alleges, "ultimately profits by any defeats which theology may sustain." To this system—variously, though in his opinion less correctly, described as Agnosticism, Positivism, or Empiricism—he gives, for reasons with which he deems it unnecessary to trouble the reader, the name of Naturalism.

Some regret may, I think, be felt that the grounds on which this important classification is made are not stated; for obviously Agnosticism is not quite the same view of the world as Positivism, and each of these as a philosophical theory has to do with considerations which are hardly recognised by pure Empiricism. The three theories are not in the same plane of thought, nor are their exponents concerned with the same issues. The Agnostic tells us that, in matters of the intellect, we must suspend our judgment in regard to conclusions which we cannot demonstrate; although in science at least he saves himself from intellectual chaos by making sundry assumptions. The Positivist offers us an amalgam of the results of the special sciences, largely based on mathematics and seasoned with a strong infusion of humanitarian idealism. The Empiricist believes that the whole of our knowledge arises, in a way which he does not explain, from a series of sensations. As the three are often at variance, any name is unfair which saddles one of them with the failings of the other two. What it is, however, that Mr. Balfour attacks under the general name of Naturalism is sufficiently clear. Roughly, it is the system or scheme of thought which places the ultimate explanation of the universe in what is physical and material rather than in what is moral and spiritual. But as he develops his argument, Naturalism seems to be also taken to include the intellectual temper which he describes as Rationalism. Now if Rationalism be taken in the ordinary sense as the intellectual temper which is the outcome of Reason, and the unrestricted exercise of Reason should lead, as it has sometimes led, to a denial of Naturalism, an obvious contradiction would ensue. Whether in the later chapters of his work Mr. Balfour entirely succeeds in solving or overcoming or even in evading this contradiction, is a matter that will presently be considered.

Further, the use of the term "Naturalism" has a very patent disadvantage : it partakes of all the ambiguities inherent in the controversial use of the word "Nature." This in turn also gives rise to difficulties which the course of the argument does not altogether remove. Whether the thoroughgoing Agnostic would assent to what are described as the leading doctrines of Naturalism, namely, that we may know "phenomena" and the laws by which they are connected, but nothing more, is, I think, open to question ; and it is still more doubtful whether, in assigning to the word "phenomena" an extension of meaning which is not justified by its etymology, Mr. Balfour himself could refuse to accept those doctrines if he held by any clear and homogeneous interpretation of the word "knowledge."

Again, the fact that Mr. Balfour professes to be writing a series of Notes introductory to the Study of Theology, and not to be constructing a definite theological system, is also attended with some misfortune ; for "Notes" are matter admittedly tentative and incomplete, and the strength of foundations must always be determined by the weight of the superstructure which they are intended to bear. Towards the close of his volume we are, indeed, supplied with a clear indication of the height and the extent of the edifice which the builder proposes to erect. The general reader, who is specially invited to witness the laying of the foundations, is likely enough, if he professes orthodoxy, to applaud the process; but with equal probability his applause will be due to ignorance of what it is that the builder is actually doing. If, however, he really grasps the force and drift of the argument; if he understands the nature of the implements that are used in clearing the ground, his ideas on the subject of structural equilibrium may possibly receive a rude shock; nay, he may even come to the opinion, which much of the work will certainly leave open to him, that, so far from laying foundations, the builder is only destroying them. The plain man, I say, should he understand Mr. Balfour at all, may conceivably feel that, whatever be the creed that is to be ultimately offered for his acceptance, it is based on the blankest negation; and that where he expected to find solid ground and a clear outlook, he is left struggling in a slough of hopeless contradictions and enveloped in impenetrable mist. The rigour of this conclusion is hardly likely to be mitigated if he undertakes to read the chapter on transcendental idealism, which the author, though it is as essential to a right comprehension of the argument as any other portion of the book, recommends him to skip. Nor, finally, will his fears be in any wise allayed by certain admissions which Mr. Balfour makes from time to time in the course of his reasoning, to the effect that, after all, he finds less difficulty in satisfying himself of the insufficiency of a naturalistic creed than in proclaiming the absolute sufficiency of any other.

Such a view of the case for theology would, however, in spite of his sceptical admissions, do Mr. Balfour a manifest injustice; for scepticism, although rampant in his pages, is clearly not the attitude of mind which he is concerned to prescribe. Yet it is undeniable that the most instructive and forcible, and withal the most convincing part of his argument, is that in which he is engaged in the work of demolition. To this two-thirds of the essay are devoted. With elegance and precision he performs the task of submitting scientific presuppositions to the test of scientific method, and he shows that, judged by that method alone, they must be regarded as utterly shallow and untenable. Mr. Spencer, of course, is treated to a full share of ironical criticism; and the doctrine of the correspondence between an organism and its environment, which degrades reason into the position of an expedient for the maintenance of organic life, and reduces morality to a species of adjustment, is unsparingly ridiculed. According to this scheme of the world, says Mr. Balfour, "by the time we are all perfectly good, we shall also be all perfectly idiotic."

Nor is this all that he achieves in the way of destruction. Having demolished scientific materialism, he professes to be not a whit more successful in his attempt to extract any coherence out of philosophic idealism. In his criticism of the naturalistic hypothesis he is obviously much indebted to Green's writings; and with the philosophy there expounded, as he frankly admits, his chapter on idealism has chiefly to do. The argument that the scientific presupposition of the uniformity of nature can be established only by the aid of that principle itself, and is necessarily involved in all attempts to prove it, might have been taken straight from Green's introduction to Hume's *Treatise*. But much in the same fashion Mr. Balfour argues that no form of idealistic creed is possible other than pure solipsism. According to this theory each individual is certain only of his own existence. The world and all that it contains is his own creation. In the infinite variety of the universe all that is fixed and stable is himself, and there is no place anywhere for "science, morality, or common sense." In Mr. Balfour's opinion this theory is the natural outcome of all idealistic speculation, notwithstanding that the conclusion is one which the majority of idealists expressly repudiate.[1]

[1] Why, asks Mr. Balfour, with what may seem to the general reader to be invincible logic, should the idealist who creates his world be so little able to

Again, there is more than a doubt whether, in speaking afterwards of a Supreme Reason, he is not using the words in a sense which is unintelligible except on an idealistic hypothesis. How, then, is he warranted in destroying the kiln which produces bricks so similar to the best of his own? Possibly, indeed, the discrepancy may be accounted for by the exigencies of his task. In his attack on idealism he seems to be making an appeal to the plain man, and the appeal is so direct that Mr. Balfour can hardly be acquitted of the suspicion, suggested also by other passages, that now and then he takes delight in exalting the plain man above the philosopher; just as on other occasions, when the course of the argument renders such a process natural, it is the philosopher who is exalted and the plain man who is abased.

II

Mr. Balfour's whole treatment of Reason and Rationalism seems to me, I confess, in a high degree difficult and unsatisfactory. He denounces Rationalism as severely as he condemns Naturalism,

understand it? Why, if he reproduces "the whole ground plan of the universe," should he lose himself so hopelessly ;"in the humblest of its ante-rooms"? A full apprehension of the idealistic hypothesis, as it is presented in the writings to which Mr. Balfour refers, ought not, I submit, to leave room for this question; for the very point which is here raised is discussed at length in the first book ot the *Prolegomena to Ethics.* Green there argues that our conception of an order of nature, and the relations which form that order, have a common spiritual source.

and yet in the last resort it is to Reason that he appears to turn. He speaks of Reason as "the roof and crown of things," and as "the ground of all existence."[1] He describes the universe as "the creation of Reason," and all things as working together "towards a reasonable end."[2] His final conclusion is that no escape from our perplexities is possible "unless we bring to the study of the world the presupposition that it was the work of a rational Being who made it intelligible, and at the same time made *us*, in however feeble a fashion, able to understand it." If these statements are true, what becomes of the attack on Rationalism? How are they to be reconciled with a repudiation of the intellectual temper which looks to Reason alone as the criterion of Truth?

To ask this question is easier than to supply any adequate answer. If answer there be, it may be found, perhaps, in a distinction which, though somewhat obscurely, Mr. Balfour draws; which to the larger number of his readers cannot be very obvious; and which he might with great advantage have made more explicit. That the distinction exists is undeniable, but it is of a technical and secondary character, and may readily be exaggerated. Even though it has a claim to rank among the niceties of philosophical terminology, it has more value for the historian of thought than for the philosopher. It is, ultimately, a distinction between Reason in a

[1] Pp. 72, 75.   [2] P. 83.   [3] P. 301.

THE SCEPTICAL ARGUMENT 53

large sense, and Reason in a narrow sense; and if I am right in my view of Mr. Balfour's procedure, he identifies this narrow sense with the Rationalistic principle. What, he inquires, is Rationalism?

> Some may be disposed to reply that it is the free and unfettered application of intelligence to the problems of life and of the world, the unprejudiced examination of every question in the dry light of emancipated reason. This may be a very good account of a particular intellectual ideal; an ideal which has been sought after at many periods of the world's history, though assuredly it has been attained in none. Usage, however, permits and even encourages us to employ the word in a much more restricted sense: as indicating a special form of that reaction against dogmatic theology which may be said with sufficient accuracy to have taken its rise in the Renaissance, to have increased in force and volume during the seventeenth and eighteenth centuries, and to have reached its most complete expression in the Naturalism which occupied our attention through the first portion of these Notes.[1]

Now in regard to this definition one thing at least is clear. It is too wide. I do not envy, indeed I scarcely understand, the attitude of a man who would deprecate the free and unfettered application of intelligence to any problem; or refuse to acknowledge that, while the goal may never be attained, the attempt to reach it is the path of progress; or deny, finally, that during the last four centuries the operation of intelligence and the achievements of progress have been marked by the reaction described. To dogmatic theology the whole intellectual activity of that period has been generally

[1] P. 168.

antagonistic,—in its poetry, in its philosophy, in its historical inquiry, in its criticism, in its natural science. Call that activity by whatever name we may, few there are who can doubt that its results are beneficial; few who can question that Religion itself has gained by the change. Mr. Balfour does not deny it. "The world," he says, "required enlightenment, and the rationalists proceeded after their own fashion to enlighten it." Plainly, then, if they are to deserve the condemnation meted out to them, their fault must be more closely defined.

Nor does their critic fail at the definition. It is not, apparently, with the work done that he has a quarrel, but with the principle employed. It is not so much the result achieved that he laments as "the original vice of its method." He blames them for their inability to effect the labour of clearance and purification without also destroying much that ought to have been preserved.[1] What that vicious method was and is—for it is still in force —we are duly told. The method is the accommodation of belief to "a view of the universe based exclusively on the prevalent mode of interpreting sense-perception." It is the assumption that the kind of experience which gives us natural science is the sole basis of knowledge. This accommodation, this assumption, is, in Mr. Balfour's judgment, the rationalising spirit; and the rationalising spirit, he declares, finds its complete expression in Naturalism.

[1] P. 169.

I do not know by what facts or arguments either of these statements can be supported. As a matter of technical usage, I submit that the method which accommodates belief to the prevalent mode of interpreting sense-perception cannot properly be described as Rationalism. As a matter of historical accuracy, I venture to doubt whether the Rationalist, as such, finds his resting-place in Naturalism. The method which Mr. Balfour traces out for us seems to be more appropriate to what is known in philosophical nomenclature as Empiricism or Sensationalism; one of the systems, let us remember, which at the outset were loosely embraced under a common title. If the special form of the reaction against dogmatic theology which is selected for censure be no more than naked Empiricism, it is questionable whether the alleged effect is not out of all proportion to the assigned cause, and whether the reaction of Empiricism alone has ever been other than slight and transient.

Rationalism, I take it, in its exact sense, is not a mode of interpreting sense-perception at all, but the claim that knowledge is attainable by *à priori* reasoning, or reasoning by principles antecedent to experience; from which nothing can well be more alien than developed Naturalism. In a less exact sense, it is not only the intellectual temper which estimates by Reason alone, a temper always operative wherever men think at all; it is also, as Mr. Balfour says, the accepted designation of a movement which, although it arose earlier and is not extinct, chiefly flourished in its various forms in the eighteenth century. From some indications in his chapter on *Rationalist Orthodoxy*, it seems as if, in his censure of Rationalism, it were with this movement that he is in the main concerned, to this movement that his criticisms are mostly relevant. Its leaders, in dealing with the problems of philosophy and theology, and in attempting to arrive at a theory of society, although they disagreed in much else, were at least united in looking to what they called the principles of *Nature, Reason*, and *Common Sense* for a solution of their difficulties. In particular, they looked to the establishment, or rather the restoration, of a *Natural Religion* as a panacea both for superstition and for scepticism. They were much busied with the adjustment of the proofs of the Christianity, drawn from the constitution of man, the analogy of Nature, the harmony of all things. The truths of Reason—whatever may have been comprehended under those words—were alleged to be no less eternal than necessary. The various religions of the world were only debasements of the one primeval, natural religion, and the basis of that religion was Reason.

But if this whole movement failed—and who can doubt that for the time at least it did fail?—that was not because its leaders made too large a use of Reason, but because the use which they made was too small. Their view of facts was partial and restricted; they had little understanding for the lessons of history; they despised the phenomena of the past as artificial and accidental; they were blind to the fact that the past had brought them to what they were; that even their own invariable principles of *Nature*, *Reason*, and *Common Sense* were not ready-made and existent from all time, but, on the contrary, were the products of growth and development. The arguments which they advanced, whether they were attacking or defending the current creed, were too narrow in their scope, too unsatisfying in their appeal; although, as Mr. Balfour is ready to grant in regard to the defence, so far as they went, they were good. If we may now select, as the cause of their intellectual disaster, any one feature of the method pursued by the Rationalists of the eighteenth century, it was their worship of mere logic. For them Reason was in the main the art of demonstration; intelligence, a firm grasp of formulæ. They had yet to learn that an essential part of Reason is to know the limits of reasoning, and that many things are true which cannot be forced within the narrow bounds of syllogistic proof.

This defect of Rationalism in what is sometimes called the Age of Enlightenment is one which has led Mr. Balfour to impugn its whole procedure, and to impugn it, as I think, too hastily; for a defect may be corrected, and a system is not to be utterly condemned because a principle has been misapplied. Assuredly the intellectual temper whose watchword is Reason is destined in the end to prevail; always provided that the watchword is understood in the fullest sense; that it is accepted, for instance, much more in the application which it receives in the systems of the German Idealists than in its restricted use in the superficial speculations of the English Deists and their followers. But while a distinction may be properly drawn between these aspects of Reason, we must always remember that they differ, not in kind, but only in scope or degree; and that the contrary supposition would lead any one who entertained it into psychological difficulties of the most insuperable character.

If, as I have ventured to suggest, it is on Reason in the larger sense that Mr. Balfour finally relies, his objections to Rationalism, taken by themselves, produce an untoward result. Standing alone, I say, they might easily convey the impression that in his judgment Reason is a very subordinate, if not an inimical, factor in the appreciation of religious truth. Nor is this impression unconfirmed by the remarkable manner in which, after attacking Rationalism, he immediately proceeds to disparage Reason afresh in order to pay a tribute to another influence, which he describes as Authority. When he thus attacks Reason, has he not, we may ask, forfeited his right to demand our devotion to a Supreme Reason, unless there be some particular virtue in capital letters? If Rationalism is anathema, why does he seek a foundation of belief in order to obtain a rational and consistent view of the world? He answers, in effect, by trying to prove that Rationalism is something essentially different from the exercise of reason. It is plain, I think, that he is somewhere entangled in the ambiguities attaching to that word. Indeed, he is compelled in a note to one of his chapters to admit that he is there using the word Reason in its popular and not in its transcendental sense; but he fails to indicate the point in the course of the argument at which he passes from the one sense to the other, and, generally, how they are to be related or distinguished.

III

Authority is a word which plays a great part in Mr. Balfour's argument. What is the exact meaning which he attaches to Authority? What is this other influence which, so far as he refers to it, is in all cases contrasted with Reason? What is the agency which, as he proceeds to affirm, has the main hand in the production of belief?

Now to examine the factors which produce a belief is indirectly to examine the question whether that belief be valid. Authority is a term clothed with associations that do not, as a rule, commend themselves to a scholar seeking a valid foundation for a system. In ordinary usage it involves conscious submission on the part of the individual and the abnegation of private judgment; an attitude which is commonly regarded as unfavourable to the pursuit of knowledge, and likely on the whole to promote intellectual tyranny. We may admit that it exercises a power which is often beneficent. We may admit that the individual cannot easily elude it; that, where the great mass of mankind is concerned, there is much to be urged on its behalf. But when everything is said, Authority in its ordinary acceptation is not, and it can never be, a foundation for a philosophic creed.

Whether Mr. Balfour is using the word in this acceptation, or in some other akin to or entirely distinct from it, will presently appear. His account of the relations which he alleges to obtain between Reason and Authority opens up many questions of great interest and importance. These relations form, indeed, the pivot on which he professes to turn from scepticism to certitude. Finding no satisfaction in any theory of science or system of metaphysics, he lights upon the fact that for the ordinary man certitude is "the child, not of Reason, but of Custom." In other words, he maintains that assent to any statement is commonly produced, not by a conscious process of reasoning, but by the overwhelming pressure of such intellectual and moral forces as "education, public opinion, the contagious convictions of countrymen, family, party, or

Church";[1] or, again, by "the spirit of the age," issuing in "a psychological atmosphere or climate, favourable to the life of certain modes of belief, unfavourable, or even fatal to the life of others."[2]

Stated as a mere fact, this, of course, is indisputable. That under the dominance of some such subtle but all-pervading influence beliefs are commonly formed; that it plays a large part in their production; nay, that with the great mass of mankind it operates to the exclusion of any other influence, is, if I may say so, one of the obvious lessons of experience. Man is not, as a rule, a reasoning animal. He accepts his beliefs ready-made. In the phrase adopted from Hume, it is not Reason, but Custom, which, so far as the average individual is concerned, supplies him with conviction. It is not Reason, but Custom, which personally gives him assurance, whether about the common facts of his surroundings, or about moral obligations or scientific truths. In either case, as our author justly observes, the use of Reason leads to unsettlement. If we are less perplexed about the beliefs on which we act every day than about speculative matters remote from the general business of life, it is only, he maintains, because in the former case we are less inclined to raise doubts.

All this is perfectly true. But from the truth of it Mr. Balfour draws a remarkable inference. He asserts that this distinction between Reason and

[1] P. 213. [2] P. 206.

Custom, in the effects which they produce, is a fact of such capital importance that, if rightly considered, it must revolutionise our whole bearing towards the problems of life and the world; that, if properly applied, it must destroy the ordinary standard by which we measure truth. Now of this assertion the least that can be said is that it is disturbing. It suggests that Mr. Balfour contemplates the immediate deposition of Reason from an ancient throne, and the setting up of Custom instead. At first blush it seems to involve the sceptical contention that Custom is king. But to entertain the suggestion would do Mr. Balfour an injustice. He makes the assertion, apparently, with the object of preparing the reader for the enunciation of a theory in regard to Authority which, so far as I know, is entirely novel. The Authority which he invokes is clearly not that of a Church; still less is it that of a Book.[1] I doubt whether in the common meaning of the term it can even be said to be that of a Revelation. If I rightly

[1] If the reader has any hesitation on this point, let him turn to *The Foundations of Belief*, p. 226: "When we reflect upon the character of the religious books and of the religious organisation through which Christianity has been built up; when we consider the variety in date, in occasion, in authorship, in context, in spiritual development, which mark the first; the stormy history and the inevitable division which mark the second; when we, further, reflect on the astonishing number of the problems, linguistic, critical, metaphysical, and historical, which must be settled, at least in some preliminary fashion, before either the books or the organisations can be supposed entitled by right of rational proof to the position of infallible guides, we can hardly suppose that we were intended to find in these the *logical* foundations of our system of religious beliefs, however important be the part (and can it be exaggerated?) which they were destined to play in producing, fostering, and directing it."

understand him, he in the most absolute manner identifies Authority with those intellectual and moral forces by which, as we have seen, rather than by any conscious process of reasoning, assent is commonly produced. Authority, in a word, is Custom. Authority, he seems to say, is the sum-total of the effects exerted by education, public opinion, the influence of family, political or ecclesiastical organisation, the spirit of the age, and however else an environment of this nature may be described.

Now entertain what view we will of Mr. Balfour's argument, he is here, I submit, taking an entirely new departure. Amid all the storms of controversy which in the course of its long history have gathered round this term, it has never, I think, until now been employed in the sense which he seeks to attach to it; although religious or philosophical disputants are not, as a rule, exposed to the suspicion of being slow at devising fresh meanings for familiar expressions. Moreover, he employs it in this sense without any warning that it is new; indeed, without any indication that he himself is conscious of its novelty. An unexpected method of attack or defence may in controversy, as elsewhere, be attended with some advantage. But here at least it has one result which, whether or not it be fortunate, could easily have been foreseen. Both with those who support and with those who impugn the traditional creed in the traditional manner, a defence of Authority, coupled with an attack on Reason, is apt to convey a misleading impression; an impression which will please the one and annoy the other just in so far as it misleads. When we consider how large a part is played in religious belief by fixed associations; when we reflect on their character in the case of Authority; when we observe with what persistence Mr. Balfour belittles the claims of its historical opponent, we can scarcely be surprised at any confusion that may be caused, or any misconception that may arise, as to the real nature of his argument.

IV

But while Mr. Balfour's use of the word exceeds, I think, the permissible limits even of a paradox; while it awakens prejudices which he would in my judgment have done better to leave asleep, the point is one which I have no desire to labour, in view of the much more important subject of the relations between Authority, as so interpreted, and Reason. He describes Authority as non-rational. "Authority," he says, "is in all cases contrasted with Reason, and stands for that group of non-rational causes, moral, social, and educational, which produces its results by psychic processes other than reasoning." What those psychic processes are Mr. Balfour does not explicitly say. But he is at particular pains to deny that Reason in its ordinary sense has anything to do with them. By an ingenious illustration, drawn from the early history of the steam engine, he compares the place of reasoning in the production of belief to the action of a boy whose duty was to move the valve admitting steam to the cylinder. With every stroke of the machine the boy had to pull a string; and thus he naturally came to suppose that the most important part of the working of the machine was due to his own personal interference. In like manner, says Mr. Balfour, are we ready to magnify the share which mere reason possesses in the production of our beliefs and the manufacture of our convictions.

But does it follow that, because conscious reasoning is only one of the secondary factors in the production of belief, those which are chiefly concerned are to be denied any participation in reason? Are they so opposed to it that, even to give point and emphasis to the distinction, they may fairly be described as non-rational? This I venture to doubt. I think that the true bearings of the matter will best be seen if we revert for a moment to the steam engine. An illustration casually employed in the exposition of a theory may sometimes be turned to a critical use. No one, of course, but a pedant will demand that it shall exactly tally with that which it is meant to illustrate, or accept it as an argument; but I confess that to me at least that which Mr. Balfour employs is adverse rather than friendly to his contention. Is it not perfectly clear that the whole of the mechanism of the steam engine was originally the work of reason in its manipulation of natural forces? Is it not also clear that the revolutionary youth who spared himself trouble by tying the string to one of the moving parts of the engine was only completing the mechanism by an exercise of the same inventive reason which had previously designed all the component parts of it? Nor is the case otherwise, I conceive, with what is called Authority. Although we may exaggerate the part which present reasoning plays in the production of our beliefs, the causes, moral, social, and educational, which are mainly instrumental in the process are the creation of past reasoning. If we follow Mr. Balfour through the interesting chapter in which he sets out to determine its nature and origin and the various manifestations of its power, we cannot, I think, fail to perceive that Authority for any age is never anything more than the resultant of the beliefs of the ages which have preceded it. Authority, in whatever shape,—political, ecclesiastical, social, educational,—represents the net effect, and too often, indeed, the *caput mortuum*, of the convictions of our ancestors. But these beliefs and convictions were in their turn the outcome of a slow and protracted course of reasoning, carried back from generation to generation up to a dim antiquity. If I may give an example of theological authority, can it be disputed that the authority of Catholic dogma was built up out of the reasonings of the Fathers in the early centuries of our era, and their subsequent acceptance at the hands of those who agreed with them? Similarly, the psychological atmosphere or climate, to which Mr. Balfour attributes so large an influence in the making of our beliefs, is produced by the aggregate of the thoughts and reasonings that, by a selective process, survive from the past. So far from being non-rational, Authority is, then, in the last resort, the outcome of reason.

It is to be observed, moreover, that Mr. Balfour himself uses language altogether inconsistent with the opposition which he endeavours to establish. In concluding his inquiry into the relations between Authority and Reason, he admits that there is a simple process by which "many of these non-rational causes can, so to speak, be converted into reasons." We recognise that our parents, our teachers, the leaders of our party, and so on, are truthful persons and well-informed; and *therefore* we believe in them and in what they say. Authority, in other words, is thus converted into "an authority," and as such, says Mr. Balfour, it becomes a species of reason. Further, he is compelled to admit that reasoning has very much to do with the production of "psychological climates"; but by a piece of logic which he does not fully explain he denies that their results are a rational product. The only results, he declares, to which reason can make an exclusive claim are of the nature of "logical conclusions"; and Rationalism, he urges, to take that as an instance of a psychological climate, is not a logical conclusion, but "an intellectual temper." But surely it is a number of logical conclusions which induce an intellectual temper, if not in any single individual, then in his ancestors or in the race. That Authority or Tradition is made up, as it were, of reason, is sufficiently proved, I apprehend, by the fact that reason is constantly modifying it; nor is the change always progressive—unhappily it is often retrograde.

But while Mr. Balfour grants that many of these "non-rational causes" may be converted into reasons, there are some, apparently, to which he denies that any such process is applicable. They are the elements of belief, which by their very nature are not, and cannot be, the subject of any definite ratiocination; although, as I submit, it can only lead to misconception to affirm that they are opposed to or contrasted with reason. What these elements are will perhaps have been rendered sufficiently clear in the course of the observations on Agnosticism to which the reader's attention was asked in the preceding chapter. They are the fundamental assumptions indispensable to any system of beliefs. They are the assumptions which the experience of practical life compels us to make. In a certain sense they are satisfactions of a need. The uniformity of Nature, for instance, which, as we saw, is one of the assumptions on which science builds, and in the absence of which a scientific system would be impossible, is not only not *proved* by the facts, but might even in many cases appear to be disproved by them. Now the outcome of Mr. Balfour's discussion on the limits of Authority and Reason is the plea that it is to Authority, and not to Reason, that we must look to supply us with the elements of belief necessary to any organised scheme of knowledge in any department of thought, whether it be natural science, or ethics, or theology. But what I venture to maintain is that, if the criticism to which the argument appears open is well founded, no such hard and fast distinction can be established. The assumptions in question are assumptions which reason makes for its own safety; they are derived ultimately from the exercise of reason upon its own process. The first inquirers, the first workers in the field of knowledge, may, indeed, have been ignorant of them; just as the true artist may be said to begin by obeying the right rules unconsciously. Assumptions, presuppositions, axioms, postulates—what are they but the elements which are discovered by analysis to be a necessary ingredient of knowledge? Without them we could not avoid intellectual chaos. Their acceptance is an act of faith, which is justified by its results.

Nor does this criticism affect the rest of the argument. How, asks Mr. Balfour, are we to account for the fact that we know? That is surely a fact which, like every other, requires to be rendered intelligible. On the naturalistic hypothesis a system is offered us as rational, "one of whose doctrines is that the system itself is the product of causes which have no tendency to truth rather than falsehood, or to falsehood rather than truth," and for which, be it added, morality is a conception that does not exist. In what perplexities this hypothesis involves us; how inadequate and irrational it is as an explanation of the facts of our intellectual and moral consciousness, Mr. Balfour endeavoured to make clear in the earlier portion of his work; and whatever we may think of the alternative hypothesis, it is not, at least, absurd and incoherent at the very outset. His final conclusion, as I have said, is that "no escape from these perplexities is possible unless we assume that the world was the work of a rational Being who made it intelligible, and made *us*, in however feeble a fashion, able to understand it." Theism, in a word, is an assumption which is "not only tolerated, but actually required by science."[1] That some Supreme Reason stands behind what Mr. Balfour calls the non-rational forces of Nature, guiding them to a rational issue, is a conviction, he urges, that is "forced upon us by the single assumption that Science is not an illusion." If, he proceeds, "we have been forced to postulate a rational God in the interests of science, so we can scarcely decline to postulate a moral God in the interests of morality."[2]

[1] P. 321. [2] P. 324.

There is, of course, a very patent objection to this whole line of argument. We may urge against Mr. Balfour that if his theological assumption were treated to the same kind of destructive criticism to which he submitted the assumptions of physical science, it could withstand the assault as little as they; that, in fact, there is not a single contention in the last section of his book which cannot be destroyed by the mode of reasoning adopted in the first. But, on the other hand, it is obvious that his method may, with equal fairness, be described as a *reductio ad absurdum*. If, he says to his scientific assailant, you will not allow me my theological assumption, I will undertake to show that your scientific assumptions are also illegitimate ; and it is undeniable that if any one were to confine himself to this argument, his position would be perfectly sound, and that he could not justly be accused on this score either of superstition or of scepticism. Of course we must admit that the converse argument also holds. If the theological assumption is legitimate; if it is to be conceded on the ground that it is the satisfaction of a need, so is the scientific. I cannot, however, disguise from myself that the scientific assumption may have certain consequences, hard to reconcile with any developed system of theology. It is a difficulty which would have to be met by any one who proposed to frame a body of religious doctrine. That that is not my present purpose, I need scarcely remind the reader.

Nor is it unimportant in this connection to point out that scientific beliefs are undoubtedly possessed of a character all their own. They produce conviction of a kind different from any which attaches to the beliefs prevailing in the sphere of ethics or religion. This practical superiority of scientific beliefs, Mr. Balfour does not hesitate to recognise. He suggests that it is largely due to the fact that they are necessities of common life. But, as he proceeds to show, and as, I think, every one must admit, the difference is not relevant. It is not a difference which should lead us to erect our beliefs about the world of phenomena into a universal standard. Because such beliefs are the first to arise, whether in the childhood of the individual or in the childhood of the human race, we must not argue that they are to prevail against all the others. "The time has passed," he says, "for believing that the further we go back towards a state of nature, the nearer we get to Virtue and Truth." If we entertain the assumptions of theology with a conviction at least as deeply seated as the assent which we yield to the assumptions of science, that is because, in the one case as in the other, they are needs which require to be satisfied. In the last resort, the claim of theology rests upon the fact that it "takes account of other needs than those which we share with our brute progenitors." For if the scientific inquirer postulates a harmony between himself and the universe in respect of his sensations and perceptions, what valid reason can be assigned why the philosopher should not also postulate a harmony between his ideas of truth, goodness, beauty, and some force or meaning in the universe? Is it not human nature which ultimately supplies us with the criteria of truth, however feebly truth may be grasped, however imperfectly it may be expressed? Surely we cannot deny that, in a sense far profounder than was dreamt of by the old Greek sceptic who first said it, *Man is the measure of all things.*

Although I have ventured upon a somewhat free criticism of Mr. Balfour's method, and, in particular, of the terminology which he employs, I do not desire to convey the impression that I am in essential disagreement with his main contention. That would be far from the truth. In my humble opinion he has performed an invaluable service in reaffirming once more one of the great verities of all philosophy. The argument *from the mere fact that we know* is, I take it, the basis of his speculations; and it is, I am convinced, the final refuge from scepticism. This, in the phraseology of Kant, is sometimes called the transcendental proof from the possibility of experience; but the truth admits of being stated in language of less obscurity. No one has given it finer or clearer expression than one of Kant's contemporaries. " Everything," says Goethe, "that we call Invention or Discovery in the higher sense of the word is the serious exercise and activity of an original feeling for truth, which, after a long course of silent cultivation, suddenly flashes out into fruitful knowledge. It is a revelation working from within on the outer world, and it lets a man feel that he is made in the image of God. It is a synthesis of World and Mind, giving the most blessed assurance of eternal harmony."[1]

If Mr. Balfour held his hand at this point, his case, I think, would be sufficient. Whether the difference between his own and some form of the idealistic hypothesis would be very great, I should not ask. It might, perhaps, be said—nay, it has been said—that in such a scheme as is here shadowed forth, God would be no more than a metaphysical abstraction; religion, merely transcendental logic tinged with emotion. But for the plain man, untroubled with philosophic subtleties, He would be the Great Father and Upholder of all things. The fine passage would be peculiarly applicable in which Mr. Balfour, in the spirit of the truest philosophy, speaks of the human race, whatever be its various creeds, as "together in the presence of the One Reality, engaged, not wholly in vain, in spelling out some fragments of its message," and as travelling, though further and further apart, yet with an intellectual progress scarcely to be discerned, "so minute is the parallax of Infinite Truth."

[1] *Sprüche in Prosa: Natur iv.*

But moved by his desire to fill up the content of human needs, Mr. Balfour cannot resist the temptation to carry his argument further, and to show by brief indications that the Christian system is that which is alone adequate. The attempt to prove too much is always unfortunate, especially in philosophy; and here the attempt discloses what I venture to call the dangerous features of Mr. Balfour's method. To affirm that a scheme must be adequate which satisfies our highest needs, involves, it must be confessed, some considerable assumptions. Had they been made by an exponent of Naturalism, I find a difficulty in believing that they would have remained uncondemned. Even though man be the measure of all things, are we not sometimes haunted by the suspicion that there is an overwhelming assumption in supposing the government of the universe to be regulated, and its laws determined, in accordance with the needs of a few creatures whose whole history is a brief episode in the life of one of the minor satellites of the sun, itself but a mere speck in an infinity of suns? To assert, for instance, that the Christian dogmas must be true because they are in correspondence with certain sides of our nature which we describe as highest and best, is to give our assent to a proposition similar to that which, in his chapter on *Naturalism and Reason*, Mr. Balfour maintained to be incredible—the proposition, namely, that samples of every sort of religious and moral phenomena are to be found "in our narrow and limited world." May we not say that to describe those sides of our nature which are satisfied by the Christian dogmas as best, is to beg the question at issue? If the parallax of truth is so infinitesimal, why should one religion much more than another satisfy our ethical needs? Will any one maintain that the ethical needs of the average Christian are always and everywhere more imperious than those of the Chinaman or the Hindoo.

But we are here concerned with religion itself, and not with any particular species of creed. If the very strength of the religious consciousness makes every other expression of it than that which happens to be our own appear by comparison dull and deficient, it is assuredly no comprehensive scheme of Divine things which builds on any such distinction; nor ultimately, I believe, is Mr. Balfour's philosophy open to any charge of narrowness, whether intellectual or moral. The sum and substance of his argument is the reiteration of the words *credo ut intelligam;* although, perhaps, in a somewhat different sense from that which Anselm originally gave them; for while his sceptical admissions are many and great, it is in a mystical temper that he brings his task to a conclusion. I do not know how the reader may regard the claims of rival speculators, but to me at least there seems much to be said for the contention that Truth is a possession which the sceptic and the mystic divide between them.

CHAPTER IV

A GIFFORD LECTURER

I

THAT the position attained by the argument which has just been examined is entirely free from doubt and difficulty, none, probably, of its exponents would pretend. That almost on every side it is open to some kind of criticism is not generally denied, even by those who are most firmly convinced of its essential truth. Were this otherwise, indeed, what call would there be for so much discussion, so much apology? Theism, like all other beliefs, is an intellectual venture, based on the needs of the mind and heart; assisted, as far as possible, by argument; finally justified, it may be, by the experience of life and the world. But of discussion on the validity of the considerations which justify this venture there has always been enough and to spare.

Much of the criticism at present directed to the theistic position may be found in the literature which has grown up around the Lectures founded by Lord Gifford in the Scottish Universities. Men of great distinction, both in science and in letters, have availed themselves of the opportunity thus afforded them to express the theories to which the learning, the research, and the thought of our time have given shape. No review of the religious philosophy which obtains among us would be adequate without some reference to the books that have been written under the Gifford Trust, and if I single out those of Professor Campbell Fraser,[1] it is because no other of the Lectures, I venture to say, has presented the case for Theism in a fairer or more impartial manner. His two series of discourses are a welcome addition to an already considerable literature, if only for their critical insight and happy gift of lucid expression. The final utterance of a veteran thinker on the supreme problem of human life, which in our relation to it at last determines, as he profoundly observes, the answers to all the questions that can engage the mind of man, is of very real human interest, no matter what the solution which he may recommend. Nor is it the least of the merits of his volumes that in his discussion of the nature and the justification of religious belief he is distinguished from the great majority of his fellow Lecturers in that he treats his high theme from the point of view

[1] *Philosophy of Theism*: being the Gifford Lectures delivered before the University of Edinburgh. By Alexander Campbell Fraser. First and Second Series.

not so much of the historical inquirer as of the rational critic.

The difference is important. At a time when science and history are pursued in a spirit hostile to metaphysical speculation, and the claims of philosophy as an avenue to truth are decried, the point of view of the rational critic is apt to be overlooked. Nowadays it is the beginnings of religion rather than the complete product that are thought to be worth investigation. Doubtless as long as we are dominated by the theory of evolution, we may naturally suppose that belief can best be understood by any explanations which historical inquiry may furnish as to its origin and development. To exhibit that origin and development—to show how religion has actually taken shape—is an interesting task; but there is something in the very form of the inquiry which appears to suggest that faith and hope and the religious conception of life may be, after all, in Dr. Fraser's words, "the transitory illusion of certain stages in history." Nor is the suggestion rebutted by the answers which historical inquirers, each after his individual bent, are in the habit of supplying. The seeker after truth is sometimes told that the first rudiments of religion are to be found in a solar myth, or in some crude notion about the infinite, or in a disease of language, or in the worship of ancestral ghosts, or in the gibberings of a baboon in a thunderstorm; and sometimes, too, he is left to assume that what religion was in its first beginnings, that it has remained in its essential nature. But whether such answers contribute much or little to the elucidation of what is obscure in the early history of the religious sentiment, they contribute nothing to a right appreciation of the problems raised by that sentiment in its present stage. The religious man will apply himself, not to the origin, but to the justification of belief; and in a day when the lessons of growth and development run no danger of being underrated, there is some satisfaction in finding that this is the light in which Dr. Fraser regards his task. He is concerned to investigate belief as it is in itself; to discover how far it is "a permanent attitude of feeling and will, consistent with reason"; to ask the question, not How did it arise? but Is it true? The fundamental problem that presses for solution is whether the ultimate meaning and purpose of the universe can be in any way explained by a system of religious belief; and if that be so, whether they can be explained in a way that will satisfy human needs. It can hardly be doubted that this interpretation of the terms of the Gifford Trust is most in accordance with the desires and the object of its founder.

I do not propose to notice more than the salient features of Dr. Fraser's work, because many of the arguments which he employs will be familiar to the reader who has done me the honour to follow me so far, and others will more appropriately call for attention in subsequent chapters. The method pursued is simple. The author sets out upon his inquiry by stating in their philosophical form the three questions confronting every thoughtful man in the world into which, unasked and unwarned, he finds himself ushered at birth: What am I? What is that which I see around me? What is the power that is operative in it and in me, and persists through every change? To use familiar terms, the three questions are the problems of self, of the world, and of God. In the articulation of the final problems we thus start, in the approved fashion, from common beliefs. To those of us who reflect at all, the reality of which we form a part, and of which we are at the same time the spectators, finally presupposes, in the ordinary human consciousness, these three existences, namely, the self, the phenomena around us, and the Power which seems to animate them. The task of natural theology is, then, to inquire whether and how far these existences may be called real, and in what relation they stand to one another.

Any rigorous prosecution of such an inquiry would be tantamount to a study of the whole range of philosophy. Dr. Fraser contents himself with a brief glance at some of the results hitherto attained. Of these perhaps the most important is that which shows us how futile is the attempt to reduce any two of these three existences to the third. The history of philosophy is eloquent of the contention on which our critic dwells, that all such endeavours make for a doctrine of universal nescience; that superstition and scepticism are the extremes into which the mind naturally falls by failing to preserve the balance between the three. Out of their mutual relations most philosophical systems of the universe have, in fact, been constructed. Theories vary according as stress is laid on one or another of them. The philosopher who starts from matter as the one ultimate certainty produces a system of Panmaterialism; a system which, clear though it may be to some modern speculators, renders the cosmos absolutely unmeaning. The idealist who is assured of nothing but that he is conscious develops the creed of Panegoism or Solipsism. The thinker like Spinoza, intoxicated with the idea of God, identifies all things with God himself. The first step in the Philosophy of Theism is, then, to examine and pronounce upon each of these systems in turn. The reader who possesses any acquaintance with philosophical speculations will hardly expect to find anything new in a presentation of the theories of the universe which are covered by these or any other names akin to them; and all that Dr. Fraser does—probably all that he aims at doing—is to restate old arguments in a convenient form, with only so much of historical reference as is necessary to explain in each case who it was that first broached them, and what developments they have since undergone.

Of the treatment of these theories there is no need to say very much. To show that each of the three is susceptible of a *reductio ad absurdum* when taken by itself is not particularly difficult; or that each appears to make by its very default for the doctrine which, as old as Pyrrho, has found favour recently in a modified, but not essentially different form, under the designation of Agnosticism. If matter alone exists; or if the individual alone exists; or if God alone exists; if in each of these theories all else is mere appearance and illusion, then obviously nothing can, in any intelligible sense, be said to be known. Nor, again, as we have seen, is there any difficulty in showing that Agnosticism, in the strict meaning or application of the term, is intellectual suicide; although Dr. Fraser's way of doing so is decidedly fresh and vigorous. He draws attention to the fact, already familar to those who can rate philosophical terms at their intrinsic value, that the statement of the Agnostic position, at least in the form adopted by its chief modern exponent, involves a begging of the question at issue. When we are told that the fundamental axiom of modern science is that we should follow our reason as far as that reason will take us, and never pretend that conclusions are certain which are not demonstrable; when we are told that all statements inconsistent with the thorough application of this rule are *unreasonable*, clearly the very question at issue — namely, whether any positive assertion about the final meaning of life may be reasonable—is by implication answered in the negative at the start. The modern Agnostic sometimes asserts that there can be nothing presumptuous in an opinion which, as he maintains, was held before him by Hume and by Kant. But, as Dr. Fraser properly observes, we cannot say that Kant is an Agnostic unless one-half of his work be rejected. If anything is presumptuous, it is certainly the claim that an integral part of a philosopher's system—namely, that which deals with the phenomena of morality—may be set aside and the philosopher still regarded as an authority in a sphere in which those phenomena are of the first moment.

Nor is Dr. Fraser any less successful in showing that Hume, who has often been called the father of modern Agnosticism, found himself unable to carry the Agnostic principle into practice. It is true that at first Hume declared that he "could look upon no opinion as more probable or likely than another." As a way out of this philosophical delirium, he came in the end to what he called "a sceptical solution of sceptical doubts."[1] He admitted that in all human reasoning from experience a step was taken, and properly taken, which was "not supported by any argument or process of the understanding." This step is, in his own words, induced by another principle "of equal weight and authority with argument,"

[1] Hume's *Essays*, ii. § 5.

namely, Custom or Habit. Only by Custom, he says, do we attain to belief or faith in a certain order and regularity in experience. That is to say, when we seek to interpret experience, we bring to the task a faith in uniformity. What else is this but that postulate of the uniformity of Nature which, as we saw in our examination of Agnosticism, reason is compelled for its own safety to maintain? There are, indeed, few writers so well fitted as Hume to offer a solvent to the inquirer, beset with Agnostic doubts, or to help him to face the spectres of the mind with equanimity. Those who quote the philosopher will do well to bear in mind what he said of his own reasonings: "Though I throw out my speculations to entertain the learned and metaphysical world, yet I do not think so differently from the rest of the world as you imagine."

II

These, however, are only preliminary considerations. The gist of Dr. Fraser's argument resolves itself into the very pertinent question whether the religious or moral "leap in the dark" is any more irrational than the leap which is taken in every species of induction in the physical or material world. Why, it may asked, should we arrest our faith at this point? He makes some lucid observations on the harmony which is involved in the fact that nature is interpretable; that our minds are successful in fathoming and anticipating the laws or sequences which prevail in the physical order. To some of the minor issues which are raised in the course of his argument objection may, perhaps, be taken, on the ground that they display a desire to prove, or even to assume, more than the data warrant. There are passages here and there in which hope and faith are brought very nearly into line, and treated as of similar validity, with beliefs which admit of demonstration, or at least of verification. But what is the starting-point, the main principle, the cardinal fact, on which Dr. Fraser takes his stand? Stated in the simplest terms, it is the fact that the universe into which we awake in becoming conscious is interpretable; that this universe is cosmic and not chaotic. Now the important question is whether, when once we have grasped this fact in all its significance, we are not compelled to go further. Must we not admit that there is some relation between our intelligence and the sequence of phenomena in which we recognise order? Can this orderly sequence be said to argue some Power or Agent operating in a manner comprehensible by our intelligence, and therefore in a sense akin to it?

That a Force of some kind exists, appears, I think, to be a necessary assumption, unless matter is to supply an ultimate explanation of its own motion. Doubtless we are accustomed to speak of natural causes. But no very profound philosophical analysis is required to convince us that the very idea and meaning of the word *cause* is imported into matter from without; that the idea is reached only by reference to personality. The motion of one set of molecules may, indeed, appear to be connected with the motion of another set; but who can fathom the connection within the sphere of matter alone? No motion can be ultimately intelligible apart from the conception of a Power which is not itself matter; and the fact that such explanations of matter and its movements as we can furnish are the product of the reason which awakes in consciousness, points to this reason as being the deepest revelation of the final truth which is within our reach. Conscious intelligence may thus be described, in a very real sense, as "the light of the world."

On the question of causality Dr. Fraser dwells at great length, because it is on this that his main argument rests. The argument, although somewhat abstruse, admits of being stated in simple terms in the ordinary language of every day. We may perhaps state it best by asking what we mean when we say that any antecedent is the cause of any consequent. All that we can perceive is a certain sequence. The so-called Laws of Nature to which science gives expression áre no more than the mode in which phenomena appear to us to be connected. In other words, the knowledge which we have is only of the connections of phenomena. Now these connections are not causes, but only the symbols of causes. Our business, therefore, is to interpret the symbols; and the very attempt to interpret them involves the assumption, it is argued, that the sequences of nature are the manifestation of intelligence. To put the matter in Dr. Fraser's language :—

> Each finite thing and finite person is so connected with every other, in the past and in the distant, that a complete knowledge of each is possible only to omniscient intelligence. Accordingly, unconditional certainty, or an absolute knowledge of the natural causes and ends of the things that are presented in our experience, is unattainable. Yet human life rests on the faith that a working intelligence, on our part, of the intelligence that is expressed in the orderly sequences and adaptations of nature *is* within our reach; so that in intellectual intercourse with the intellect that is latent in Nature our human intellect will not in the end be put to confusion. When we try to interpret nature as sense-symbolism, we often find our hypothetical interpretations verified by the event; and although there is for us no demonstrable certainty that with innumerable unknown causes in existence what has been now verified will be undisturbed, this faith sufficiently sustains us. This is that faith in the harmony between the course of nature and the thought of man which, as we found, was the last word even with Hume. . . . May we not therefore assert that in our surrounding universe we are continually in the presence of a Power that reveals itself in articulate language of law and purpose?[1]

The outcome of the argument, take it as we will, is that Nature is governed by a mind ultimately akin to the human mind. Now of this conception the least, I think, that can be said is that it presents a great many difficulties. Some of them recur with the conception of a design or purpose immanent

[1] *Philosophy of Theism*, first series, pp. 239, 240.

in Nature, and we may, perhaps, more conveniently discuss them in that connection in the following chapter. The argument also involves the doctrine, enunciated by Berkeley, that natural causation is essentially divine. This has always appeared to me, I confess, as a restatement of pantheism. Indeed, Dr. Fraser admits that the constant divine determination of Nature is the truth which theism may be said to have received from that theory. But if this constant divine determination is to issue in a thoroughgoing pantheism which reduces all things, good and evil, order and disorder, truth and error, to so many manifestations of a divine unity and necessity, we are confronted with a fresh difficulty. What account, we must ask, is to be given of the raw material in and through which this divine causation works? Are we to hold, for instance, with some philosophers, that God was and is limited in respect of certain physical data? Or are we to agree with Dr. Fraser when he seems to suggest, in a later utterance, that the problem he has raised is quite insoluble? "Natural causation," he observes, "in its ultimate implicates, and morally responsible agency in its ultimate implicates, are both alike *incompletely* intelligible, at the scientific point of view." From this he argues that neither of them can be proved to be so related to the other as to be incapable of a mutual reconciliation under some higher principle. I do not know that this last reflection is very consoling, for the simple and familiar reason that inability to prove a negative is not the same thing as proving an affirmative. Beset by so many perplexities, a man might well conclude that the course least open to objection is to take refuge in hope, and cheerfully commit himself to that "leap in the dark," whether in things physical or moral, which, even as Hume recognised, is "a species of natural instinct."

Theism, according to Dr. Fraser's view, is the result of many converging lines of argument. It might, I submit, be more appropriately described as a simple postulate—a conviction which the nature of experience renders necessary. The question at issue is whether or not we may reasonably accept a morally perfect power as the foundation of the physical, æsthetical, and spiritual experience of mankind. Does this hypothesis provide the sole escape from the paralysis of sceptical despair? Does it offer a more satisfactory explanation of a greater number of the aspects of life than any other, or rather than universal doubt, the only other possible alternative? If the idea of infinity which attaches to the universe awakens in the last resort both doubt and faith, is the one or the other to be triumphant according as this infinity is regarded from an atheistical or a theistical point of view?

That there are many obstinate difficulties in which these issues involve us, it is idle to deny. The whole philosophy of religion is there to prove their existence. If they form for the sceptic the embodiment of his doubts, for the theist they are equally the province in which his faith is exercised. There is the difficulty, for instance, of reconciling the conception of a morally perfect Power, an omnipresent Being, with any conception that we can form of personality. Can God be intelligibly described as a Person? Is not personality something finite, individual, particular. How, then, can personality be omnipresent? I do not know that any very convincing answer has been given to this question. The theistic apologist commonly maintains that the special character of a *person* is not individuality or definite embodiment, but simply *moral relation;* that the special character of a *thing* is *mechanical or physical relation ;* and that if we are to treat the universe as an object of moral faith, that object must be the revelation of an infinite Person. Dr. Fraser adopts this answer. The language in which he expresses himself suggests that he does not recognise any other form of existence than can be conveniently covered by the two names *person* and *thing*. Possibly, however, he would not refuse to admit that in certain aspects of theism God might be designated as simple power, or law, or love, or justice; in respect of which theistic belief would be less open to the charge of anthropomorphism, or at least of anthropopsychism—of making God in man's own image—if He were described as a *quality*. Some degree of anthropomorphism, we must candidly confess, seems an inseparable element in the theism which finds its ultimate source and justification in man's moral nature.

This is a difficulty of the intellectual kind; and even the physical world has intellectual difficulties which no exercise of human reason can solve. But the chief difficulty in the way of theism is of a moral character. What account can theism give of the problem of evil? How can it reconcile the pain and suffering of the world with the existence of an omnipotent and benevolent God? Is there anything new that can be said by a modern apologist on this perennial question? If, to use the language of Dr. Fraser's work, natural causation is essentially divine, what is to be said of the causes, sufficiently numerous in the world, which appear to conspire together for evil? To judge by certain allusions in the *Philosophy of Theism*, the reader is left to infer that it is intellectually possible that agents are present in the universe who are responsible for what ought not to happen. But such a statement as that does no more than put the difficulty further back; we are compelled to ask, Who, then, is responsible for the presence of such agents? Again, the reader might suppose, from another allusion, that the problem of evil is to be overcome by a faith or trust that evil is concealed good. This faith or trust is hard to reconcile with some of the facts of life as we know them. Their repulsive nature seems to make rather against than for the adoption of any such creed. That this problem is the real crux of the theistic hypothesis, and the chief difficulty which it presents to the human mind and heart, scarcely requires demonstration ; nor can any apologist find a more useful application of his eloquence and acumen than the task of showing that the existence of evil is not in itself a ground for refusing to adopt that hypothesis. To say that Dr. Fraser has solved the problem would be like saying that he has squared the circle or discovered a method of perpetual motion. The problem, he frankly confesses, does not admit of solution in the strict use of the term. It offers, he says, an insoluble difficulty to any purely empirical philosophy. The difficulty is not to be overcome, but only to be reduced and mitigated.

What are the considerations, then, which may deprive this problem of some of its terrors? There is the reflection, to begin with, that without an ethical or theistic trust empirical philosophy is itself paralysed. The ultimate mysteries of causality, the final riddles of natural science, are in themselves every whit as dark as the moral problems presented by the pain, the suffering, the injustice, and what theologians call the sin and guilt of the world. As we have seen already, science is not possible, nor its procedure even intelligible, without some form of faith—without the hypothesis that Nature is uniform ; that the man who trusts her will not be put to intellectual confusion. Reduced to plain terms, Dr. Fraser's argument is that if the universe may be held to be intellectually trustworthy, it may, with at least equal reason, be held to be morally trustworthy too; that morality as well as science is incomplete, and the theory of both is unworkable, without the faith that all life is of divine constitution; and that the man who trusts the power which is darkly revealed in life will not in the end be put to moral shame. We are brought back, by a different path, to what may be called the argument from scepticism. The final sanction for the theistic hypothesis, as applied to the explanation either of the physical or of the moral world, is that without it we are reduced to a condition of unreason and despair, in which, as we can know nothing, so on the other hand we can hope for nothing; that knowledge in the physical, and hope in the moral world ultimately rest on the same basis; and that atheism, to be consistent, should deny the possibility of both.

If cosmic faith is the assurance that the material world will not in the end put to *intellectual* confusion those who rely on the universality of its natural order, this blended moral and religious faith not only guarantees the physical faith itself, but is the *absolute* assurance that the Supreme Power will not put to permanent *moral* confusion those who strive permanently to realise the ideals of truth and beauty and goodness; or who trust absolutely in infinite love, in and through which all things somehow work together for good to those who thus love.

And again :

When Bacon speaks of man as the interpreter of nature, only so far as he is its *obedient minister;* and when he makes the suggestion in the often quoted words, "Natura non *nisi parendo* vincitur," does he not strike the key-note of reverential submission to an authoritative voice, proceeding from the reality that is undergoing investigation, and which must not be gainsaid, although it is only imperfectly comprehensible, accepted at last in an act of obedience rather than of victorious intelligence. And is not a like idea at the root of the memorable words, "If any man will do His will he shall know"—know by this practical criterion—the final difference between individual opinion and the divine reality—know this so far as this is intellectually comprehensible by man. Not through intellect alone, or by man exercising himself as a thinking being exclusively, but in and through the constant exercise of all that is best or highest in him—through the active response of the entire man, while still in an incompletely understood "knowledge"; it is only thus that it is open to man finally to dispose of his supreme problem, with its mysterious intellectual burden. The final philosophy is practically found in a life of trustful inquiry, right feeling, and righteous will or purpose—not in complete vision; and perhaps the chief profit of struggling for the vision may be the moral lesson of the consequent discovery—the consciousness of the scientific inaccessibility of the vision.[1]

Now the essence of this doctrine of faith is that the appeal is made only to those who, in some degree at least, share the faith. That that circumstance is any serious objection to the validity of the doctrine, or takes away from its inherent value, who of us will venture to affirm? We do not reproach the Artist because the appeal which Art makes is only to those who, in some degree at least, are endowed with a sense for what is true, beautiful, or significant in life. And has not Art, equally with Religion, its mysteries that cannot be solved, its aspirations after a never attainable Ideal?

[1] Second Series, p. 133.

According, then, to this philosophic faith we find the germ of theism in the ethical root of life and the spiritual ground of the interpretability of experience. In the threefold articulation of real experience from which we started, theism of this kind is the unifying and harmonising principle. If the existence of evil be held to be in irreconcilable conflict with this principle, an Agnostic pessimism would seem to be the only alternative to belief. There are, of course, other explanations of the problem of evil which from time to time have found favour. There is the hypothesis of Manicheism that the universe is the battlefield of two rival and eternal powers, one good, the other evil. There is the orthodox theory that the whole human race has fallen from a Divine ideal as the result of temptation by a malignant spirit called the Devil. But neither of these explanations will fit into any philosophic estimate of things, because in either case the difficulty is only put further back and aggravated. The Devil himself has to be explained, and the inevitable transmission of sin to be justified. To argue, again, that evil is an unconditional necessity in a finite world of individual beings, or in a world that was of necessity formed of pre-existing matter, is beside the mark; for evil would no longer be immoral if it were necessary—if it ceased to consist in what ought not to be, and were transformed instead into what cannot but be.

These and similar attempts to explain away the

existence of evil are commonly considered nowadays to be unworthy of serious consideration. Whether they compare unfavourably with some other theories which, with a scarcely greater show of reason, have been suggested in their place, is not altogether certain. One of these theories is that of the existence of a Devil, in which, perhaps, few thinkers believe. Yet it is idle to deny that the existence of a Devil is an hypothesis which would explain a very large number of facts in a very effective manner. A dispassionate survey of human nature and the course of history might suggest that there is at least as much evidence of his existence as of God's. But in modern times philosophers have apparently agreed to abandon the Devil as a working hypothesis, and they offer us as a solution of the problem a scheme which seems to make evil the result, not of the operation of a mischievous personality, but of failure to pass, so to speak, a certain examination. It may, we are told, be a sign of perfect goodness that men should be placed in this world on educational trial with an absolute power to make themselves bad and so remain. Dr. Fraser speaks of this with great reverence as a Divine experiment in personal responsibility, and suggests that, even though failure be sometimes—might he not have said most often?—the result, this scheme of things is a better one than a wholly physical, non-moral, and necessitated universe. He appears also to suppose that even omnipotence cannot exclude the existence of evil, so long as there are beings whose characteristic is that within certain limits they are endowed with freedom of choice—a characteristic which he sums up by calling them persons. I do not think that this argument will command any permanent approval. Surely there is a contradiction in speaking of omnipotence as unable to prevent beings so endowed from exercising their freedom to choose evil instead of good. That is as much a limitation of the Divine perfection as any of those attempts to explain away the existence of evil which were found to be so unsatisfactory. Omnipotence, of course, might create beings who would always choose good, even after temptation; and a God at once benevolent, omnipotent, and omniscient, such as theism supposes, must, so far as the light of human reason extends, be regarded as abrogating one of His attributes in the creation of beings who choose evil.

That any such solution of the problem of evil as we have considered lies open to this criticism is, indeed, obvious. There remains the solution suggested by simple faith—the trust

> that somehow good
> Will be the final goal of ill.

But here what argument is possible? This trust, I venture to say, is part of the natural creed of mankind; and if the philosopher attempts to justify it, can he do else than return once more to his contention that the religious "leap in the dark" is as legitimate as the leap which is taken in every physical induction? To prove that contention he must deal, however, with a consideration of some weight, which, with many minds, destroys the value of the analogy. Any physical induction, we may say, is capable of verification, of direct and cumulative testimony to its truth; but where is the verification of the theory that, in the last resort, a world which seems so full of unmerited suffering and triumphant wrong is morally trustworthy? The truth of the induction that all men are mortal is attested afresh every hour; the theory that the universe is morally trustworthy, that every wrong is somehow righted, seems as frequently to be demolished by hard facts. If this objection can be answered, it will be, I imagine, by the logic, not of the schools, but of life. Experience, perhaps, rather than any process of reasoning may force the conviction upon us that it is more rational to hold that the universe is morally trustworthy than to accept the necessary alternative, and abandon the human mind to the suicidal belief that morality is a delusion. What, we may urge, can mere dialectic avail if it be the last conclusion of practical wisdom that, even though there be an irremovable residuum of mystery in the problem of evil, there is still sufficient room for faith and hope? After all, as Dr. Fraser maintains, an Agnostic pessimism could rest only upon a complete perception that the existing universe must necessarily exclude all grounds for the religious temper. By its very nature the whole question can be decided only by a balance of probabilities. If the general experience of mankind should turn the scale in the end in favour of a theistic optimism which leaves many things unexplained, that would be a fact which no philosopher could afford to neglect.

Dr. Fraser is too well aware of the connection commonly assumed between theism and the alleged evidence of design in nature to leave the subject undiscussed, and one of his most interesting chapters is devoted to this connection. In its bearing on theistic belief the teleological argument, as it is called, has always exercised some appeal; but none, perhaps, has been so completely transformed by the progress of scientific theory in our own time. I propose to offer a few observations upon the argument in the shape which it takes in a recent work by the Duke of Argyll, and to a brief consideration of that work I now invite the reader's attention.

CHAPTER V

TELEOLOGY

I

THE argument that the phenomena of Nature exhibit marks of design, and are therefore the work of an Intelligence, has been from the earliest days of speculation the commonest of all the so-called proofs of theism. Socrates appears to have defended it. Cicero wrote a treatise on it. Paley made himself a name by putting it into popular form. In the *Critique of Pure Reason* Kant speaks of it as "the oldest, the clearest, and the best adapted to human reason; as giving life to the study of Nature, inasmuch as it derives its own existence from Nature, and thus constantly acquires new vigour." He declared, too, that the argument would always deserve to be treated with respect, and that any attempt to diminish its authority would be futile. Yet in a few trenchant observations he showed that the conclusion to which it is supposed to lead is not contained in the premises.

Other modern philosophers, both before and after Kant, have similarly condemned it; and if a *coup de grace* were needed, this the argument may be said to have received at the hands of Darwin. But in the place of the old teleology there has arisen another; not, indeed, new—since it had its beginnings among the Greeks—but very different from that which it has dislodged. If the reader is to grasp the essential distinction between the two, he will do well, before considering the claims advanced by the second, to reflect for a moment upon the inconclusive character of the first.

To begin with, the utmost, as Kant pointed out, that the argument from design could establish would be an *architect* of the world, always very much hampered by the quality of the material with which he had to work; not a *creator*. We should still have to ask, Whence came the material, and why was it made to assume a shape which presents so many difficulties to a designer? There is no parallel whatever between the construction of a machine and the creation of a universe. Design implies the conception of a Power overcoming hindrances, and how can an Omnipotent Being be so conceived?

Then again, the observed marks of alleged design do not necessarily point to a designer outside them, acting independently of them, and able to modify them when and how he pleases. They may be the expression of immanent law following on the conditions of the matter in which they are observed, and, as Darwin showed, on the conditions of the environment. When we affirm that any set of movements has a certain end, all that the affirmation implies is that the movements were sufficient to produce that result; and the result may be just as logically maintained to be the necessary outcome of the movements as to be the end which they were designed to effect. We may also urge that design implies some element of choice, and there is no evidence that any choice existed.

Further, the observed effects are finite; and we have no warrant in logic for inferring that they proceed from an Infinite Cause. They would never of themselves have suggested an Infinite Cause, and to maintain that that is what they prove is only to advance a conclusion which has been already assumed.

If any other consideration be required to show that the old teleological argument is invalid, we need only call to mind the innumerable imperfections that meet us everywhere in the world. If there is design anywhere, it must exist everywhere; the good and the evil must be alike designed. No reason can be given why one phenomenon should be specially selected, and many others ignored. Universal design, extending to the observer himself, is hardly to be distinguished from mechanism. On this point, indeed, something more is to be said hereafter. But if design exists in the world at all, there seem to be so many conflicting designs at work that the most reasonable conclusion to reach would be that there are numerous designers in partial or complete antagonism one with another. This, however, would hardly be a proof that could be advanced in support of theism.

Now the new teleology frankly abandons this search for evidence of mind in particular contrivances, and endeavours to view Nature as a whole, and to consider whether there is any such evidence in what are called its laws. The most popular of the recent statements of the new teleology, although not without some traces of the old, is to be found in a work by the Duke of Argyll entitled *The Philosophy of Belief; or, Law in Christian Theology.* The Duke here makes an attempt to develop the arguments which he set himself to expound in *The Reign of Law.* That treatise, which was published more than thirty years ago at the height of the commotion raised by the Darwinian hypothesis, discussed the question whether physical laws were to be accepted as the final and supreme agency in nature, or whether those laws were not rather, in their essence, manifestations of an omnipresent mind, which was thus brought within the grasp of human intelligence. The inquiry there begun was taken up afresh in a later work. *The Unity of Nature* professed to investigate the competence of the human mind itself to form any trustworthy judgment on this question. While the first volume attacked that purely materialistic and mechanical conception of the universe which seemed to receive support from Darwin's speculations, the second was an energetic protest against the Agnostic philosophy revived by some of his disciples. In the *Philosophy of Belief* the Duke applies the results which he has previously reached; he endeavours to establish a connection—nay, even a harmony—between the idea of an omnipresent mind in nature and the highest teachings of Hebrew and Christian theology; and thus to bring himself into line with that reaction towards a reasonable faith which is not the least remarkable feature of contemporary thought.

There is nothing in this last work which is more calculated to impress an intelligent reader, and, if he is given to speculation, to astonish him, than the note of certainty which everywhere pervades it. Although the author touches in his pages upon a great number of subjects of immeasurable difficulty, which have exercised the acutest intellects of all ages, he does not appear to labour under any very grievous burden of diffidence. It has often been observed that the love of religious argumentation is peculiarly characteristic of the Scotch, and it is no less true that north of the Tweed argumentation is more ready to issue in dogmatic assertion than elsewhere. In this respect the Duke of Argyll does no dishonour to the national genius. He writes with an air of easy assurance which may well be the outcome of perfect conviction, but may also suggest, at any rate to less fortunate philosophers, that he has unduly disregarded some of the perplexities which attend upon a coherent creed. In an interesting preface, partly of an autobiographical character, while he admits that he has never had any scholastic training either in theology or philosophy, he expresses some confidence that the reasoning which he has pursued will be of the same use to others as he has found it to himself; and he bases this belief on the fact that the first of his treatises has had a very wide circulation, and also on the contention that, as far as he is aware, the work was never met by any attempt at refutation or reply. Doubtless he is justified in assuming that the views which he expresses in this volume will exercise as great an influence as those which he put forward in *The Reign of Law.* It is written with the same lucidity and force of style, the same wealth of apt illustration and pregnant suggestion, as distinguish all his writings. In its copious eloquence alone it is a remarkable achievement for a man who has passed the allotted span of human life. Style, an abundant diction, and a tone of easy confidence are, of course, good things in themselves, and when a wide popularity is added to them will mould great masses of opinion; but they afford no guarantee that the treatise which they adorn opens up any really new vein of thought or makes any solid contribution to the settlement of the vexed questions that beset us.

The Duke of Argyll's main position is that in

Christian theology we are presented with a system of thought which rests upon a firm ground of ascertainable fact. What he maintains to be an ascertainable fact, "as susceptible of proof as any other," is that a mind, offering not only close analogies with our own, but obviously of the same kind and quality, is everywhere operative in nature. "The ubiquitous presence of this higher agency is," he says, "not a matter of inference alone, but is an object of direct and immediate recognition."[1] He urges that the most remarkable proof of the fact may be found in the uses of human speech, which fails to offer any adequate description of natural phenomena without recourse to words and expressions indicating the existence and the influence of mind.

That nature is governed by mind is an ancient conception—so ancient, indeed, that, as the Duke observes, it has probably had much to do with the origin of all mythologies; and in that ordinary and, it must be added, unreflecting speech of every day to which he makes an appeal, the conception still holds its own as an easy and obvious solution of certain problems. But to argue from the common use of language that some sort of design is at work is a process of a very suspicious character, even though the language be employed by philosophers. For what is language but the set of counters or symbols by which thought is expressed?

[1] *Philosophy of Belief*, p. 5.

That its terms and uses are largely metaphorical is a notorious fact, which might put the least philosophic of men on his guard, and prevent him from supposing that because we are accustomed to speak of natural phenomena as though they were guided by mind, they are therefore so guided. Moreover, it is only to such of these phenomena as seem to present some resemblance to human agency—and in comparison with the vast whole they are infinitesimally few—that any attempt is made to apply a theory of adaptation. May we not say, indeed, that there is a Fallacy of Design not any less erroneous than that Pathetic Fallacy in which poets and romancers excusably indulge? We are pleased to cherish the fancy that Nature sympathises with our emotions; nay, that she herself is swayed by emotions like our own. Bright skies, we may imagine, are evidence that she has a part in our joys; clouds and gloom, that she shares our sorrows. We speak of a storm as threatening; of a howling wind as melancholy. But even a poet is aware that these are fantastical conceits. If Nature, then, cannot be said, except by mere metaphor, to act in any accordance with our emotions, have we any greater warrant for supposing that she acts in accordance with our thoughts? If in order to express her phenomena in the terms of our chief vehicle of thought we are forced to attribute to her a mental process analogous to that which we should attribute to ourselves, that circumstance is no proof, is not even a presumption, that she is endowed with a mind in any way similar to our own. So much for the argument from the use of language.

A brief review of the history of the conception that nature is governed by mind would have been in place in a disquisition on its philosophical importance, and might not, perhaps, have been without a beneficial effect upon the course of the Duke's speculation. His method, however, is not historical. Now and again he does, no doubt, indulge in a retrospect, but seldom with any illuminating result as far as the difficulties of the conception are concerned, and, once or twice at least, with curious consequences. For an exponent of the theory of divine ordination in nature to appeal to the conclusions of Epicurus and Lucretius is on the face of it somewhat rash. If there is any doctrine which sums up and characterises the philosophy of Epicurus, it is that everything has a natural cause, and that it is the clash of primeval atoms, and not any divine guidance, that governs this world. To say that that philosophy is "entirely spiritualistic in its ultimate conceptions" is surely a strange perversion of the views of a thinker who held that matter is the universal substance, that mind is a mere accident, and that if there are any gods at all, they exist far off, careless of mankind. Even as applied to the professed poetry of Lucretius the statement is quite unaccountable. The Duke would have been better advised if he had gone back to the pioneers of Greek thought; for there he might have found that one, at least, of those neglected speculators not only formed the conception that nature is governed by mind, but in seeking to give the doctrine a philosophical shape also unravelled some of the difficulties attending it. Anaxagoras, like the Duke of Argyll, assumed an ordering mind as the original moving force of the world. In two respects, however, he was unlike his modern colleague. He considered the distinction that must exist between that mind and the ultimate matter with which it had to deal, and in which it was presumed to work. He was also content to abide by mechanical causes where they appeared to be sufficient. When he came to carry out his conception he found himself beset with difficulties, for which, as the Duke will remember, he was twitted by Plato in the *Phædo*, and even by Aristotle, who nevertheless admitted that, compared with earlier philosophers, he was like a sober man among drunkards.

We might, I say, have expected that in a modern work written to maintain this conception, some of the elementary difficulties of the position would be discussed; and, in particular, the difficulty of formulating any intelligible relation between the operative mind and matter itself. Either mind is to be separated from the material in which it works, or it is not. If it is to be so separated, what account is to be given of the material? How did matter come into being? In what way, if at all, does it limit or restrain the action of mind? If it does limit that action, as seems to be inevitable, how can mind be the manifestation of a Being whose powers are presumed to have no limit? On the other hand, if mind is not to be separated from the matter in which it works, "mind" and "nature" become convertible terms; nay, they become indistinguishable. This hypothesis reduces us to what must be called either a purely pantheistic, or, from another point of view, and with the use of other terminology, a purely materialistic interpretation of the universe. If the Duke were compelled to choose between the horns of this dilemma, he would clearly refuse the alternative that led to pantheism; for, if there is one statement in his pages more decisive than another, it is that "pantheism is essentially materialistic, leaving no natural or consistent place for spiritual things." We can hardly be wrong, then, in crediting him with the other assumption. But to the obvious difficulties of this assumption he does not appear to pay much attention. Possibly they are included in the intellectual perplexities which, as he observes here and there, beset the application of his main thesis; but so inextricably are they bound up with it, so profoundly do they determine its value and validity, that a writer who professes to deal with the philosophy of a belief in it can hardly win support for his opinions if he does not discuss them to the full.

II

But be these difficulties what they may, they do not, in the Duke's opinion, even remotely affect the certainty of the conception on which he takes his stand, that nature displays the operation of a mind analogous to our own. I confess that to me, at least, the evidence for that conception—or, as the Duke will have it, for that ascertainable fact—is far from being of any very sure or convincing character. Such evidence as is alleged to exist is drawn partly from recognition of certain laws in nature, and partly from the marks of design which nature is supposed to display. On the subject of design sufficient, perhaps, has already been said to show that no argument based upon it will carry us very far on the road to theistic belief. The Duke does not make any serious attempt to turn the edge of the general objections which, as we have seen, may be urged against his view. He might with some propriety, for instance, have referred to the part which the Darwinian hypothesis has played in weakening the teleological argument as it has hitherto been understood. But he does not do so. He goes no further than the mere assertion that if natural selection has any meaning at all, it implies a mental and directing choice. Undoubtedly some kind of choice seems to be implied in the word; but zoologists, I suppose, would meet the objection by pointing to this as an admirable example of the use of metaphor. To assert that the process which is thus described as selection implies the operation of a mind, is the very question at issue; and certainly the question may be more easily begged at the outset than argued. The problem to be solved is whether the world presents to us a system of means adapted to ends; and if that be so, whether we have any right to say that this adaptation is evidence of mind. Can we ever be certain that the means, or, in other words, matter and its changes, would not themselves have issued in the result which we call their end? Design, of course, may exist, although we cannot prove it. When the Duke relies on design as an incontrovertible evidence of the existence of mind, he is, I think, relying on what is, at the best, only a possibility, and a possibility which can be transformed into a probable hypothesis on any wide scale only by an act of faith. But who would venture to assert that in this case faith and probability render any strong support to theism? Even though it be granted that the world exhibits design, the evidence is by no means uniformly in favour of the existence of such a Being as God is represented to be in the scheme of Christian theology. Nature, as we saw a few pages back, might well seem to be the theatre in which many mutually conflicting designers were at work. At times it exhibits features which might lead us to infer that it was intended to promote the misery of all sentient creatures. The human body, for example, might be said at certain moments to be a most cunningly devised mechanism for the infliction of needless, useless, and inexplicable suffering. What sort of a God would it be of whose mind such design was evidence? The truth is that the argument from design will establish the existence of the Devil quite as convincingly as that of God, although I confess that I am not familiar with any writer who uses it for that purpose.

Now if the argument from special contrivances breaks down, what is to be said of the other source from which the Duke draws his conviction? What is to be said of the theory which sees evidence of mind in the general arrangement of the universe? Upon this point we shall do well to remember that the contention that what we call the laws of nature are evidence of mind does not, in the strict sense, involve a teleological theory. By itself that contention has nothing to do with the doctrine of final causes; that is to say, it does not assert that the end to be attained is a determining factor in the sequence of phenomena. But, as will immediately appear, it is the foundation of what I have described as the new teleology. We must first, then, examine the contention as it is in itself; or, rather, as we find it stated. Can the laws of nature be urged as a proof for theism? On this fundamental question the Duke leaves us in no doubt as to his opinion.

He tells us that the only conception which will solve our difficulties is

> the conception that what we call natural laws, both in the physical and in the moral world, are indeed Divine, owing their origin and all their unchangeable authority to some inseparable relation to the character of the Almighty, to the issue of His will, of His righteousness, of His truth.[1]

Further, the whole of *The Philosophy of Belief* is eloquent of the contention that of the mind which is thus at work in nature we have a direct and intuitive perception. This mind is declared to be obviously of the same kind and quality as our own.

Against any such view there is much to be said. In the first place, as regards the laws of nature, the Duke does not always write as though he had sufficient grasp of the truth that "law" in this sense means nothing more than an observed order of phenomena. It is unquestionably a most important fact that the human mind and the order of nature are in some way and to some extent correlated — that the succession of events in the outward world is in an intelligible harmony with our ideas, or some of them. As I have shown in a previous chapter, it is, in my humble judgment, the fundamental fact from which all theistic reasoning must start. But we are not logically justified in going further, and in asserting that because our minds are adequate to the comprehension—or, to speak more accurately, the very partial

[1] *Op. cit.* p. 333.

comprehension—of some of the processes of nature, therefore nature must be governed by a mind like our own. That that mind is like our own is not an ascertainable fact, but a pure assumption; it is not an intuition, but an exercise, if we will, of faith.

For other explanations are possible. We may take Kant's statement that "the understanding makes nature," and interpret it in the sense that the mind which we see in nature is merely the projection of our own. The order which we observe may also be the expression of a merely mechanical necessity. There is nothing to show that either matter itself or the order which it exhibits ever had any beginning; and every mind of which we have any experience has had a beginning. Again, the inference that ability to interpret nature brings man's mind into close approximation with God's is quite invalid; for it assumes without any evidence at all that the laws in question, as we know them, are the only possible interpretation of the great complex of phenomena to which we refer them. We may hold that these laws, which are no more than the sequence we observe, are only special aspects of matter visible to finite eyes and intelligible by finite minds, and that some other interpretation, differing from ours not only in extent, but in kind, might be put upon them by God. To exclude the possibility of this conception is to make God entirely in man's own image. There is nothing to warrant us in arguing from our scheme of science to His scheme, or in assuming that our minds are in any way correlated with His.

Nor is this all. Apart from the tremendous assumption here made, it may be specially objected to the form in which the Duke makes the assumption, that when he declares law to be the expression of some supreme agency, he is using "law" in the sense, not of an observed order, but of cause. He is supposing that law is some external force controlling phenomena, rather than some succession immanent in and inseparable from them. For if he uses "law" in its legitimate sense, and still maintains that the laws of nature may be identified with the operation of God, it is clear that he is not far from the pantheism which he so vigorously condemns.

But the laws of nature can have no meaning for us apart from nature itself. The question, then, whether these laws are the expression of mechanical necessity, or of something that we can call mind, resolves itself into the more general and ancient question whether it is mechanism or intelligence that finally governs the universe. Now, in regard to this question, it is important to remember that the mechanical and teleological conceptions are not mutually exclusive. They may exist side by side. The mechanism may even be regarded as the means by which the purpose is wrought. If the province of science is the investigation of the mechanism, the object of philosophical inquiry is to determine what account, if any, may be given of the purpose. There is nothing in the best scientific opinion of our time which is in conflict with this view, or has established any thesis which tends to make a teleological conception of nature impossible. In his essays on Darwin's work and influence Mr. Huxley, for instance, gave unmistakable assent to it.

The Telcology which supposes that the eye, such as we see it in man or one of the higher *Vertebrata*, was made with the precise structure which it exhibits, for the purpose of enabling the animal which possesses it to see, has undoubtedly received its deathblow. Nevertheless, it is necessary to remember that there is a wider Teleology, which is not touched by the doctrine of Evolution, but is actually based upon the fundamental proposition of Evolution. That proposition is, that the whole world, living and not living, is the result of the mutual interaction, according to definite laws, of the forces possessed by the molecules of which the primitive nebulosity of the universe was composed. If this be true, it is no less certain that the existing world lay, potentially, in the cosmic vapour; and that a sufficient intelligence could, from a knowledge of the properties of that vapour, have predicted, say the state of the Fauna of Britain in 1869, with as much certainty as one can say what will happen to the vapour of the breath on a cold winter's day.[1]

That mechanical interpretation is not irreconcilable with the existence of purpose is, indeed, so obvious as hardly to require statement. Philosophy, equally with science, recognises that nature is susceptible of a teleological interpretation. In one of his later works, *The Critique of Judgment*, Kant, notwithstanding his earlier views, declared

[1] *Darwiniana*, p. 110.

that a teleological interpretation was not only possible, but also necessary. Nay, he went further; he maintained that a teleological sense was as real and inevitable as reason itself; although as little as reason could it penetrate to the essence of things, and as little as mechanism could it express that essence. Possibly, he urged, a free and absolute intelligence would perceive that ultimately the teleological and the mechanical interpretations are identical; but as far as man is concerned, the very constitution of his mind compels him to look upon the whole of nature as a product, and the very idea of that product as the cause of its possibility; in other words, as its end. He cannot divest himself of the conviction that the mechanism of nature is subservient to some design.

The contention has often been raised that purpose seems to be involved in the very notion of an evolutionary process, by which, out of the motion of the primeval atoms, all that exists is brought into being, the less perfect gradually yielding to the more perfect. Now if the primeval atoms were to undergo any development, one thing, at least, appears to be clear: it is impossible to conceive of them, even on a purely mechanical theory, as not endowed with the forces necessary to produce that development. Such an admission even the most punctilious exponent of science can, I apprehend, have no hesitation in making. But the contention to which I refer is raised, as a rule, not by him, but by the philosopher anxious to settle accounts with science. Although a full discussion of this subject would carry us into the remoter regions of metaphysical speculation, and involve us in difficulties of which no ready solution is available, the real question at issue is of no particular subtlety. In its most intelligible form it is this: Is there any aspect of the whole evolutionary process which, from the purely scientific point of view, is a manifestation of distinct purpose? I venture to contend that there is such an aspect, and that it is to be found in what is known as *the struggle for life.* Of the new terms coined in the statement of the Darwinian hypothesis none has attained a wider currency than this; none has been oftener used to impose a mechanical interpretation upon nature. Now whatever opinion may be held as to the precise teleological significance of the struggle, it must, I think, be conceded that teleological significance of some kind there undoubtedly is. For although the term in its scientific meaning is merely a metaphorical expression for the ceaseless influence of environment, under which such varieties as are best suited to it, or best protected by it, tend to survive, can we reasonably assert that the fact of their survival is wholly explained by mechanical conditions? Are mechanical conditions a first cause? Surely not. They may shape the struggle, but plainly there would be no struggle at all if, underlying it, there were no vital impulse, no persistent effort, no will; or, to employ Schopenhauer's language, if *the will to live* were not the fundamental fact. Here, indeed, I may appeal to what has been said by a leading exponent of the modern theory of evolution. In his *Natural History of Creation*, Haeckel admits that in ultimate analysis what determines the struggle for life is self-preservation. Now what is self-preservation but effort directed to an end? What, then, does the struggle for life mean but *the struggle in order to live*, and does not this in itself give a teleological character to nature?[1]

I do not know how the matter may present itself to the reader; but for my own part I confess that the argument seems to indicate a means of reconciliation between theories that are commonly thought to be hostile to one another. From this circumstance we must be careful, however, to draw no unwarrantable inference. Even though we may be forced to put a teleological interpretation upon nature; even though that interpretation may point in some incomprehensible fashion to the action of intelligence upon matter, it is, as we saw in the last chapter, no more than a postulate that this Intelligence is akin to our own; or that the universe for us, to use Dr. Fraser's language, is intellectually trustworthy. We cannot, I make bold to maintain, go beyond the assertion that it is

[1] This point has been very succinctly put in Professor Alfred Weber's *History of Philosophy*.

a postulate which the nature of experience renders necessary. Between that postulate and what is commonly called theistic belief, there lie all the considerations already mentioned, affecting the theory of a mind operating in nature and the moral character of that mind. These are considerations which generally fail to receive their due weight at the hands of theistic apologists like the Duke of Argyll, who are more concerned with the development of a thesis than with the attempt to reconcile it to the facts of life. The greater part of *The Philosophy of Belief* is devoted not to philosophical or scientific questions, in the strict sense of the words, but to an account of the main aspects of Hebrew and Christian theology. On this latter subject the author writes with a fervour and a sincerity which would make the fortune of a hundred preachers. He discusses the character of the Godhead as conceived by the prophets and singers of Israel, and in no recent work do the ethics of Hebraism receive a better or more vigorous treatment. He discourses, with a welcome tolerance for liberal theories, on the varying aspects of the Messianic idea. He treats of faith, sacrifice, inspiration, and regeneration in a way that to intelligent Christians can hardly fail to be interesting, even though it may not always commend itself as a complete solution of difficulties. Finally, he enlarges on the nature and foundation of Christian ethics, the theory of prayer, and Christian belief in relation to philosophy. But in the last chapter he returns from these discussions to take up again the thread of the argument with which he began. He expresses, with undiminished assurance, his unalterable conviction that Christian theology "has its feet firmly planted on the common and solid ground of ascertainable fact and corresponding law." Nay, more: in so many words he identifies nature with the will of one supreme Law-giver, whose character is perfect love and righteousness and truth.

A fervid faith, however, is one thing—possibly the best thing; and philosophical argument is another. It is philosophical argument which the Duke professes to supply; but he does not, I submit, grapple with the difficulties which any philosophy worthy of the name is bound to consider. He does not, any more than other theologians, succeed in the attempt to reconcile the benevolence and righteousness of God, whose will is nature, with the cruelty and injustice which, in any human view of morality, nature constantly displays; so far is he, indeed, from succeeding in the attempt that he can hardly be said even to make it. The fatherhood of God, the brotherhood of man, and a kingdom of grace, are the primary doctrines which Christ taught. In what way can they be reconciled with the ascertainable facts of natural law? How can they be based upon an observed order in which not love or pity, but the murderous competition of all sentient creatures, reigns supreme?

The plain truth is that, in spite of the harmony between mind and some aspects of nature, any attempt to derive a satisfactory religious creed from the contemplation of merely physical phenomena, after the fashion of the Duke of Argyll, is, if I may venture to state my opinion, essentially perverse. It involves a confusion between the physical and the spiritual which, under the plea of reconciling science and religion, is hurtful to both. If religion is not entirely a matter of faith, but requires, and is susceptible of, a philosophical proof, it is in the region of spiritual and moral rather than of physical phenomena that such proof is likely to be attained.

III

The confusion of which I speak never, perhaps, received more abundant illustration than has been provided in our own time by some of the writings of the late Professor Henry Drummond. They were curiously unequal in value. For the manuals of edification which he composed in a style not less admirable than simple, as also for the blameless character and high example of his life, I entertain no feeling but that of the most sincere respect. He accomplished, I have no doubt, a vast amount of good; and to pass any severe criticism on any one of whom so much can be said is scarcely an agreeable task, particularly when the subject of it is removed from the sphere of our small controversies. But Professor Drummond was also the author of two or three books dealing with problems of science in a manner which cannot, even by any generous exaggeration, be described as scientific. If I refer to these books here, it is only because of the immense popularity which they seem to have enjoyed and, for aught I know to the contrary, may still enjoy. Of a treatise in which he endeavoured to show that natural law was as applicable to what may be called the spiritual aspect of the world as to the physical I do not propose to say anything; but I invite the reader's attention to some brief observations upon a later work, *The Ascent of Man*, as the argument there advanced is in some respects germane to the subject of the present chapter.[1]

From the confident tone adopted in the opening pages of this work we might suppose that some important scientific discovery was about to be given to the world. Professor Drummond described his task as "an attempt to tell in a plain way a few of the things which science is now seeing with regard to the Ascent of Man." His starting-point was, of course, the theory of evolution; but he proceeded to assert that those who had hitherto treated of that theory had conceived it amiss. His theme was

---

[1] There are indications in a recent biography of Professor Drummond that towards the close of his life he himself came to perceive a fundamental error in the position adopted in his *Natural Law in the Spiritual World*. Nor are there wanting further indications in the same work that some of the views expressed in the *Ascent of Man* might have undergone a development which would have surprised the friends of his youth.

the ascent of man, the individual, during the earlier stages of his development.

> So far [he said] as the general scheme of Evolution is introduced—and in the Introduction and elsewhere this is done at length—the object is the important one of pointing out how its nature has been misconceived, indeed how its greatest factor has been overlooked in almost all contemporary scientific thinking. Evolution was given to the modern world out of focus, was first seen by it out of focus, and has remained out of focus to the present hour. Its general basis has never been re-examined since the time of Mr. Darwin; and not only such speculative sciences as Teleology, but working sciences like Sociology, have been led astray by a fundamental omission.

In short, he charged the philosophy of evolution not so much with ignoring man, for of that error, he admitted, it had seriously begun to repent, as with "misreading Nature herself." Although many great men have been at work reconstructing the cosmos in the light of evolution, there was, he protested, hardly one of them who had any perception of the true scientific point of view.

Unless I am much mistaken, the reader will look in vain for anything to justify these words; nay, from a dispassionate examination of the sequel to them he can hardly fail to arrive at the conclusion that Professor Drummond possessed an ample endowment of that quality which friends and admirers may, perhaps, have described as courage, but which those who fail to admire will call by a harsher name. What, then, is this missing factor in current theories? Besides the struggle for life, now commonly "accepted by the scientific world as the governing factor in development," what is this "something else at work" which we have hitherto failed to recognise?

There is, in point of fact, a *second* factor, which one might venture to call the *Struggle for the Life of Others*, which plays an equally prominent part. Even in the early stages of development, its contribution is as real, while in the world's later progress—under the name of Altruism—it assumes a sovereignty before which the earlier Struggle sinks into insignificance. That this second form of Struggle should all but have escaped the notice of evolutionists is the more unaccountable since it arises, like the first, out of those fundamental functions of living organisms which it is the main business of biological science to investigate. The functions discharged by all living things, plant and animal, are two in number. The first is Nutrition, the second is Reproduction. The first is the basis of the Struggle for Life; the second, of the Struggle for the Life of Others. These two functions run their parallel course—or spiral course, for they continuously intertwine—from the very dawn of life. . . . Yet in constructing the fabric of Evolution, one of these has been taken, the other left.

Those who remember the character of Professor Drummond's speculations in his *Natural Law in the Spiritual World* will find no difficulty in understanding the use to which he put this "second factor." He was a writer—I trust I may say so without offence—who was particularly exposed to the dangers of sentimental rhetoric. He took the doctrine—which, if not exactly as old as the hills, possesses at least a very respectable antiquity—that society and the moral sentiments which give it stability had their rise in the family; with this he combined the well-known account of the origin of altruism long ago elaborated by Mr. Herbert Spencer; and he then proceeded, by an entirely false analogy, to speak of altruism as a "Struggle for the Life of Others" based on the physiological function of reproduction, and comparable in force and effect with the "struggle for life" in the state of nature. Following upon this, he descanted at length on the part played by the "Struggle for the Life of Others" in the economy of the world. Finding what he described as "the opportunity of evolution" in the act of birth, and declaring that "our first and natural association with the Struggle for the Life of Others was with something done for posterity — in the plant the Struggle to produce seeds, in the animal to beget young,"—he read ethical implications into every form of reproduction which he could find in nature, and committed himself to a series of the most extraordinary confusions, of which the following may serve as an example :—

> The first chapter or two of the story of Evolution may be headed "The Struggle for Life"; but take the book as a whole, and it is not a tale of battle. It is a Love-story.

And again :—

> Every plant in the world lives for others. It sets aside something, something costly, cared for, the highest expression of its nature. The seed is the tithe of Love, the tithe which Nature renders to Man. When Man lives upon seeds, he lives upon Love. Literally, scientifically, Love is Life. If the Struggle for Life has made Man, braced and disciplined him, it is the Struggle for Love which sustains him.

That a work written in this style and professing to "readjust the accents" in the theory of evolution, should be popular, is sufficiently conceivable. There is, therefore, all the more necessity for indicating, in a plain fashion, some of its errors. Professor Drummond declared that his discovery had all but escaped the notice of contemporary men of science; whereas he borrowed the discovery from their speculations. In speaking of "the Struggle for the Life of Others" as based on reproduction, he cannot, I think, be acquitted of having perverted the meaning of the word "struggle" as commonly understood by naturalists. That the function of reproduction is intimately associated with the struggle for life, in the proper sense of the words, must be perfectly obvious. When a writer refers to the struggle for life as "based on nutrition," we can hardly fail to suspect that he has never really grasped its meaning; and here the suspicion is confirmed by a stray allusion to the *Origin of Species*. In that publication, said Professor Drummond, Darwin "offered to the world what purported to be the final clue to the course of living Nature." Now although the reader will doubtless be familiar with the purport of so famous a work, yet for the sake of a clear understanding of the matter I shall venture to point out that all that Darwin tried to do was to explain why living things fall into certain groups with certain characters and relations. He found an explanation in the struggle for life, based not on nutrition, but on the three facts of variation, heredity, and indefinite multiplication, and their interaction with the influence of the environment; with the result that the forms best adapted to the environment tend to survive. The "struggle for life" is, as I have said, simply a metaphorical name for the process which ends in this result. If Professor Drummond had properly understood so elementary a truth of modern biology, he could not have spoken of the struggle for life as being determined by, or dependent on, nutrition. I am, indeed, at a loss to know what he meant by the phrase, unless it be that waste of tissue is repaired by taking food; but that is not a proposition which requires a series of lectures for its due establishment.

Again, without the grossest abuse of language, altruism cannot be described as a struggle, nor is there anything in its working at all analogous with the working of the struggle for life. To say of a flower which scatters, perhaps, a thousand seeds that it is engaged in a struggle for the life of others may be a pleasing fancy. Erasmus Darwin, it is true, wrote about the loves of plants. But statements of the kind are poetical; they have nothing whatever to do with science. Professor Drummond, in rightly observing that maternal care and sympathy is a condition of existence in the infancy of all the higher animals, proceeded to declare that any species which neglected this "altruism" was extinguished in a generation. But if, as he wished to maintain, this

" Struggle for the Life of Others " is from the very
dawn of life intertwined with the "Struggle for Life,"
what explanation could he have given of the survival
of the cod and the herring? Would he have described the production of spawn as an altruistic or
ethical process? Or is an oak to be considered as
"other regarding"—as a moral agent—in the moment
when it sheds acorns? Or can either of these
operations be fairly described as a " struggle"?

To follow Professor Drummond through all the
statements in his pages to which objection must be
made, would overtax the reader's patience; but there
are one or two more which may, perhaps, be usefully
noted. He stated that the inheritability of acquired
characters was an assumption of Charles Darwin's,
whereas the doctrine in reality belongs to Erasmus
Darwin and to Lamarck, and Darwin's own opinion
on the subject seems to have changed more than once.
He complained that the naturalist does not consider
man in all his aspects in the scheme of evolution, and
he described the root of the error as lying with
the author of the *Origin*. But Darwin was perfectly
well aware of the scope of his theory in 1859, as
may be seen by the concluding words of that work;
and for the last thirty years a host of writers have
been engaged on every possible aspect of the human
animal. Nor is it correct to say that the theory in
question was developed mainly in connection with
the humbler phases of life. The gradations of
structure in the higher animals, and especially

between men and apes, played the largest share. Further, it might seem from a passage in which he declared that evolution gives the human mind "a new dimension," as though the doctrine of evolution were not one of the oldest and earliest of scientific speculations. Again, he talked of "life being controlled by its functions." The functions of an organism are the operations which it performs; in other words, they are the expression, and the only possible expression, of its energy. How, then, can energy be controlled by its own manifestations? Professor Drummond tried to explain the purport of his words by referring to the functions of a locomotive engine, but that made matters worse; for, as the function of a locomotive engine is to propel itself, it is impossible that that propulsion can be described as controlling the engine. What he doubtless wished to establish was that the purpose for which he supposed life to exist was operative from the beginning of life and directed its development; or, in Aristotelian language, that the initial cause of life is identical with the final one, whatever that may be. Lastly, he spoke of the reproductive process of self-division in a cell as though it were actually carried out, not as an organic necessity, but "in pursuance of the Struggle for the Life of Others"; whereas a little later the account which he gave of this process makes the reproduction of the cell directly dependent on the function of nutrition.

Christianity has often been pronounced to be the

perfection and fulfilment of all other religious systems; nor have there been wanting philosophers who have also pronounced it to be the perfection and fulfilment of all systems of philosophy. But not until our own day has any writer attempted to make Christianity entirely congruous with nature. In the last pages of *The Ascent of Man* the reader is informed that

> up to this time no word has been spoken to reconcile Christianity with Evolution, or Evolution with Christianity. And why? Because the two are one. What is Evolution? A method of creation. What is its object. To make more perfect living beings. What is Christianity? A method of creation. What is its object? To make more perfect living beings. Through what does Evolution work? Through Love. Through what does Christianity work? Through Love. Evolution and Christianity have the same author, the same end, the same spirit. There is no rivalry between these processes.

I do not know whether Professor Drummond accepted the Pauline account of Christianity. But if so, I may be permitted to ask how that account can possibly be reconciled with the comparison here suggested. No one could commit himself to this comparison who was not fully persuaded that the struggle for the life of others had either completely vanquished, or was about to vanquish, the struggle for life. Of such a consummation of the cosmic process there are, I apprehend, no signs as yet.

CHAPTER VI

BUTLER ONCE MORE

IT has been said that the progress of thought has created a demand for a writer who should demonstrate that so far from the claims of religion, either natural or revealed, being overthrown by a consideration of the course of nature in the light of the theory of evolution, religion itself may best be understood by the application of an analogous theory. The argument would take some such form as the following: Religion may be unable to prove that the God whom it assumes is desirous of the welfare of all men, or that the lives of the majority are not destined to apparent waste. It may contend, on the contrary, that only the few are to attain to happiness and perfection, and to possess them at the expense of the many. It may declare that the man who is to be regarded as the fullest embodiment of moral or spiritual force is merely the victor over innumerable rivals, for whom the conditions of existence were less favourable than for him. If religion be thus unable to exhibit a God who is all-good and all-powerful, there is nothing in nature, our imaginary writer might urge, which shows that to infer the existence of such a God is unreasonable; for nature herself exhibits the same phenomena.

Whether this argument would make for theistic belief, or would constitute a veiled attack upon belief, is a question that does not readily admit of being answered. The reader who is acquainted with English theology in the early part of the eighteenth century will perceive that the argument is an old one in a new form. It is suggested for present consideration by a perusal of the *Studies Subsidiary to the Works of Bishop Butler*, in which the late Mr. Gladstone embodied his opinions on some of the great topics of which we have treated. If philosophy be valuable in so far as it is the outcome of personal experience, and the profoundest philosophy be likely to issue where the experience is widest and richest, then undoubtedly these *Studies* ought to merit our attention.

Mr. Gladstone's industry and endurance, and in an even greater degree, the perennial vigour, the unquenchable ardour, and the curious subtlety and versatility of his mind, were so well known—they so often dazzled his contemporaries, of whom he must at the close of his life have been able to reckon full three generations—that his last achievement, remarkable as it was, hardly, perhaps, excited all the astonishment which it deserved. In another man of the same years any prolonged intellectual exercise would be something exceptional and extraordinary, but in Mr. Gladstone's case it seemed to be entirely fit and in complete accord with his nature and character that at an age which few reach, or reach only to be dotards, he should have been engaged on a course of severe and profound inquiry, for the purpose of settling a final account with himself and the world on the ultimate questions of human destiny. To Mr. Gladstone, however, the inquiry was in no wise new. The fact is notorious that his devotion to theological speculation was always as great as his interest in politics; possibly, indeed, it was always greater. Friends and enemies have alike declared that if he had not risen to the highest office in the State he would certainly have been the chief minister of the Church; and had he lived in an earlier epoch of English history he would not improbably have united both dignities in his own person. Therefore, when in his latest years he published a volume the contents of which are almost wholly of a theological cast, he did no more than continue studies that were begun in youth, and in manhood were never neglected. What more worthy exhibition was ever offered of the truth of Goethe's aphorism that he is the happiest man who can set the end of his life in connection with the beginning?

The evidence of this continuity of work and thought is abundantly supplied by these *Studies*.

One of the chapters which compose them was written as long ago as the year 1830. Numerous books which have made a stir in the world since then are cited in the course of the argument, and were apparently read and studied with great care. Another chapter, dealing in brief compass with the main purpose and result of Butler's treatise, was first published in a popular review in March 1879. But the greater part of the volume was the product of more recent labour, and some of it, indeed, had first seen the light only two or three years before the author's death. While the work embraces a great number of topics, it is, as a whole, sufficiently homogeneous, if due regard be paid to the promise of the title; and whether in respect of its zeal and acumen, or its learning and research, or even the quality of the style, it presents, as a piece of literature, many admirable features. Never did Mr. Gladstone write better English or was he more successful in minimising that tendency to prolixity and mere grandiloquence which not unfrequently detracted from the force and effect of his language. His treatment is everywhere sober, dignified, and impressive. On the highest of themes there is scarcely an exaggeration in saying that in places it is majestic.

These *Studies* are intended to be subsidiary to an edition of Butler's "Works" which Mr. Gladstone gave to the world. They fall into two parts.

The first treats at large of the method as contrasted with the argument of the *Analogy* and the *Sermons;* on the application of the same method to the Bible; on various points in the teaching of those works; on their history and influence; and, more especially, on the criticisms to which they have been exposed. The second discusses the subject of a future life, sketches the development of opinion and provides a summary of the chief theses which have been entertained with respect to it. The teaching of the bishop on the question of a future life gives the point of departure. Similarly, texts are found in various references to these topics for chapters on necessity or determinism, teleology, and miracles. Doubtless these topics are not so prominently connected with the substance of the bishop's writings as to render a discussion of them indispensable; but, as his champion was well aware, they underlie the bishop's position, and must be investigated by any one who sets out to determine the general questions to which his argument ultimately leads, and the intrinsic value and outcome of his contribution. They also serve an interesting purpose in disclosing the nature of Mr. Gladstone's own views and the exact limits of his philosophical speculations.

In his lucid account of Butler's method and general characteristics Mr. Gladstone showed himself not insensible of the fact that much of the direct argument of the *Analogy* is commonly held to be antiquated, or at least to be no longer adequate. Although he did not admit that any such allegation was true, he confessed that the highest importance of the work is to be found, not in its argument, but in its method. If the distinguishing feature of Butler's method is that in dealing with facts of an indeterminate character, such as moral and religious phenomena, he applies the doctrine of probability more clearly than any other writer, the encomium is well deserved. But the value of the method lies in its application, and its application here is the argument advanced. The reader will remember that the *Analogy* was written to confute the Deists. Butler met them on the ground that was common to them and himself. They admitted a religion of nature, and, in particular, the chief doctrine of that religion—the doctrine, namely, that the universe was created and governed by a ruler at once almighty and benevolent. That was a conception which was seen then as now to involve a great many difficulties; but these they steadily ignored, maintaining, in the words of Pope's famous dictum, that "whatever is, is right." A religion of revelation, however, they denied; and they based their denial on the contention that there the difficulties were such as to deprive the religion of all credence. Butler argued that revealed religion presented an exact analogy with nature; that the difficulties in either case were the same or similar. Thus he had an easy task in convicting his opponents of a radical inconsistency, in bearing with the one and cavilling at the other.

We cannot, however, affirm that because Butler was able without much effort to overcome the Deists on their own ground, his own position was impregnable ; and what Mr. Gladstone undertook was to defend him against the censure to which his argument has been subjected by various critics. I do not propose to enter minutely into the objections to the general scheme of the *Analogy* which these critics have advanced, or to examine in any great detail all the pleas by which the objections are sought to be met. To do so would be to carry the reader's attention away from the question to which these pages are devoted, and to ask him to pursue certain lines of personal or historical interest which, although sufficiently attractive in themselves, and bearing in some degree on the main problem, do not go to its centre. Nor shall I pretend that I have any very high opinion of the manner in which the critics of the *Analogy* are confronted. On some minor points, no doubt, the defence is successful ; but where great questions are involved, the method employed is not of a kind to carry conviction in the times in which we live. While it is throughout sustained with a fine display of dialectical ingenuity, little hesitation is shown in having recourse to ecclesiastical dogma when arguments fail. In other words, the defence, from the point of view of the unbeliever, is abandoned.

Mr. Bagehot urged, with great force, that we might expect revelation to explain the difficulties to be found in the religious interpretation of nature, and not to add others of its own. We may admit that the objection strikes at the very heart of Butler's argument. Mr. Gladstone tried to turn the blow by replying that Mr. Bagehot mistook the seat of the evil, which lies not in the darkness of the understanding, but in the perversion of the will; that the speculative difficulties involved in revelation constitute, in Butler's view, the chief test and discipline of those to whom such difficulties appeal; and that, in general, it is for the practical necessities of life that religion provides. The logical conclusion of this argument would be that revelation is addressed to the will rather than to the mind of man, and possibly Mr. Gladstone was of that opinion. Possibly, indeed, it may be the right opinion. But the fact remains that Butler's argument is directed to the solution of those mental difficulties; and if appeal is made to reason, the decision must not be rendered null and void by asserting that reason is distorted and darkened by passion. So much for the answer to Mr. Bagehot.

To Miss Hennell and other writers who complain that the *Analogy* raises more doubts than it solves, and conduces to scepticism, the only reply that was attempted to be made was that Butler appears to be fully conscious of this objection;

further, that, as regards the facts of nature which feed the sceptical tendency, he meets the objection by deriving them from the original corruption of the world. He is aware, said Mr. Gladstone, that in defending religion by the contention that it only reproduces difficulties with which we are familiar in the constitution and course of nature, he casts a weight upon the back of nature itself. But he holds that nature is well able to bear the burden, and that the things which have been objected to in nature may, in a certain light, be perfectly consistent with wisdom, justice, and goodness. Here again, however, if the appeal be made to common facts, it must be decided by those facts as they are. To invalidate the appeal beforehand by declaring that the objectionable facts are the outcome of corruption, or that things may be consistent with wisdom and goodness which, as far as we can judge, are obviously the reverse, is manifestly unfair.

A defence of Butler conducted on these lines will hardly please Mr. Leslie Stephen, whose criticisms on the *Analogy*, to be found in his *English Thought in the Eighteenth Century*, were next examined. Mr. Gladstone charged him with confusing the two essentially different processes of rebutting and proving; but that is a charge which in some degree attaches to Butler's argument itself. Mr. Stephen's objection to the argument of the *Analogy*, whatever else may be said of it, is hardly,

I think, open to any criticism on the score of obscurity. "No evasion," he declares, "can blind us to the true bearing of Butler's statement: God made men liable to sin. He placed them where they were certain to sin. He damns them everlastingly for sinning. This is the road by which the *Analogy* leads to Atheism."[1] Mr. Gladstone's answer to this is that the objection, if true, does not lie specially against anything in the *Analogy*, but is an objection to the whole body of Christian Theology. Undoubtedly it is, if it is true. Mr. Gladstone went further. He described the objection as striking at the whole body of theistic belief. The only answer which he provided was that of the mass of evil in the world by far the most was due to man's abuse of the free agency with which he has been entrusted. But what more is meant by free agency than liability to sin? While the stroke and counter-stroke, though sufficiently definite, are given in an issue technically, indeed, outside the special province of the *Analogy*, unquestionably they are of vital moment to its argument. They involve the whole problem of evil.

The reply to Mr. Matthew Arnold's criticisms, which are too loose and unimportant to deserve statement, is conceived in a vein of mingled banter and contempt. This, I am unable to deny, is mostly well deserved, if only on account of the very magisterial, not to say dictatorial, airs

[1] *English Thought in the Eighteenth Century*, i. 301.

which Mr. Arnold was fond of assuming on questions admitting of a great variety of opinion. Nor will I trouble the reader with the manner in which Mr. Gladstone defended Butler from the strictures of a number of minor critics, and from two common charges which were accustomed to be made against him, namely, that he was not Evangelical in his views, and that his system favoured Popery. All that need be said is that the attitude of defence did not blind Butler's apologist to certain points (most of them of restricted interest) on which he was undoubtedly open to criticism. A list of questionable theses advanced by him is drawn up, and several features of his metaphysical creed are adversely scrutinised. Mr. Gladstone's zeal and ingenuity led him, however, to offer some defence for the statements in question, by representing that they were adopted from contemporary thought, and that if the bishop had examined them with the insight usually characteristic of him, he would have withheld his countenance.

Not the least interesting part of Mr. Gladstone's labours is the account which he offered of the influence of Butler's works. He disposed, with great zest and satisfaction, of the tradition which attributes to Pitt the common saying that the *Analogy* raises more doubts than it solves; and he contrived to throw a fresh light on the character and attainments of Lord Chesterfield by selecting a passage from his writings which, as he declared, represents Butler's dominant ideas in the shortest compass, and tends to show that his speculations were sufficiently well known in 1752 to be familiar to that cultivated man of the world. But nothing in the influence of Butler on particular individuals is more worthy of notice than a confession which Mr. Gladstone made of himself in recording that, to his mind, there is no preparation for the satisfactory study of Butler so good as to have been widely conversant with the disappointing character of human affairs.

As to the philosophical questions of which, in his remarks on necessity or determinism, on teleology and on miracles, Mr. Gladstone treated, there is room for an even wider difference of opinion than is aroused by his defence of the *Analogy;* but few competent judges will quarrel with the assertion that his grasp of the bearings of these questions leaves much to be desired. The controversy between the advocates of free-will and the Determinists, or—as Mr. Gladstone preferred to call them—the Necessarians, is hardly to be decided by the arguments which he used, or the authorities whom he accepted as representative of the rival contentions. Nor, again, is the subject of teleology to be adequately discussed in these days without taking large account of the speculations of Kant and of Darwin. There is not the slightest indication in his pages that Mr. Gladstone had ever given any serious attention to Kant, and his familiarity with the application of the Darwinian hypothesis appears to have been extremely limited. A large part of his observations under this head are in connection with a volume by the late Mr. Romanes, dealing primarily with religious phenomena. For a comprehensive statement of the argument from physical adaptation he referred his readers to the Bridgewater treatises, as though they still represented the best that has been said and thought on the subject. Nor can I believe that he fully apprehended the drift of Hume's argument in the matter of miracles. He had, indeed, little difficulty in showing that what is described as a miracle in one age may in another be referred to a law of nature, or an application of a law of nature, previously unknown. But he argued as if Hume had declared that miracles were intrinsically impossible. What that philosopher declared was that in the existing state of human knowledge they are incredible ; that if human testimony in a single instance contradicts a known law of nature, it is more probable that the testimony is false than that the law has been in that instance reversed. With Hume, as well as with Butler, probability, as we perceive, is the guide of life ; but he applies the principle with a difference.

Mr. Gladstone went so far as to confess that Butler's work, adjusted as it was to the needs of his own day, is inadequate to the needs of ours. His argument does not, he said, of itself confute the Agnostic, the Positivist, or the Materialist. On this point, however, I venture to say—and the reader who has had patience with me so far will understand the grounds of the statement—that to the Agnostic, at least, the doctrine of probability finds a very appropriate application, and that Mr. Gladstone could have materially strengthened Butler's claims on the attention of modern readers if he had devoted some pages to this aspect of his teaching. If the Agnostic who is not a Pyrrhonist fails, as we have seen, to carry his suspense of judgment into the region of natural phenomena; if, like Mr. Huxley, he admits that in that region a probability so high as to amount to practical certainty may be attained; if he is confidently assured that nature will not betray him, is there any valid reason why the doctrine of probability should not be applied in the region of moral and religious phenomena also? Has the doctrine any less restricted scope in the one than in the other? In a treatise on Butler that professes to correspond to modern needs, questions of this character might usefully have been discussed; for, as has been observed, it is to Butler's method rather than to his argument that the chief interest of his work must now be assigned.

Mr. Gladstone might also have done something to estimate Butler's true position in the history of philosophy. Had he done so, he would not, perhaps, have found a difficulty in understanding why that distinguished writer has exercised no appreciable influence outside the limits of his own country. But in spite of omissions, in spite also of certain shortcomings in his scheme of defence, we cannot, I think, doubt that he performed for Butler's work a great and lasting service, and that he has imparted to us something of the same sympathy which he himself entertained for the qualities of his author—"a sympathy with candour, courage, faith, a deference to the Eternal, a sense of the largeness of the unseen, and a reverential sentiment, always healthful for the soul, towards the majestic shadows with which it is encompassed."

CHAPTER VII

ROMAN CATHOLIC WRITERS

I

ALTHOUGH it is no part of my purpose to enter upon a discussion of any of the common creeds which are based upon theistic belief, there is no disguising the fact that with the vast majority belief, in any reasoned form, is not the foundation, but, on the contrary, is the product of these creeds. In other words, belief commonly rests, not upon any conscious exercise of intelligence, but upon submission to the teaching of a Church, which is regarded as the sole depositary, or at least as the guardian, of truth. Theism, the argument would run, is tenable because the Church teaches theism among other dogmas. We shall, therefore, do well to cast a glance at the kind of argument by which in our day submission to ecclesiastical authority is sought to be justified; and there will be some convenience, for this purpose, in taking the authority claimed by the Roman Catholic Church as at once the most conspicuous and coherent. As I do not suppose that I shall be honoured by the attention of many readers within that communion, the selection of the Roman Catholic Church will have the additional advantage of providing a purely objective example of the kind of argument in question. The objection may be raised that in the form in which I shall deal with it the argument is advanced, not by the recognised teachers of that Church, but by laymen, and that neither in importance nor in popularity is it comparable with any of those which have hitherto been examined. But these circumstances do not make some reference to it any the less expedient in a general review like the present.

The Roman Catholic writer seeks, of course, to show that submission to the Church is demanded by the plain dictates of reason. This is the procedure, for instance, adopted by apologists like Mr. W. S. Lilly,[1] who in an interesting volume published a few years ago stated that his object was to inquire whether the Christian religion is tenable from the point of view of those who are practically outside its pale. He described his inquiry, in so many words, as in the nature of an *argumentum ad hominem*, undertaken for their benefit. The argument is addressed, he says, to "a great and growing multitude of cultivated and virtuous men and women," honestly unable to use the old religious symbols;

---

[1] *The Great Enigma.* By William Samuel Lilly.

and he seeks to show them that, on the very principles which they especially prize, Christianity claims and demands acceptance.

Now amongst the principles which cultivated and virtuous men especially prize is, or ought to be, a clear definition of the terms to be used. There are so many kinds of Christians that Christianity has become a vague and elastic term, and the interest, not to say the success, of the inquiry materially depends upon what it is that is meant by Christianity. If, however, as is here the case, the object of the inquiry is to persuade, we must allow the advocate the fullest liberty to state his argument as he thinks fit. Of the arts of persuasive rhetoric none is commoner or apparently more effective than to keep back the object to which the rhetoric is directed until a proper pitch of enthusiasm has been reached. Accordingly, we must look to the concluding pages of *The Great Enigma* for an exact account of the point with which the whole of it is concerned. While approval is there bestowed on the rotatory statement of Dr. Johnson that Christianity means the religion of Christians, the author does honestly proceed to remove any doubt as to the sense in which he employs the word, or as to the end and aim of his persuasive process. He defines Christianity as a theology, the life of which consists in dogma. He exhibits unfeigned contempt for those who profess Christianity without accepting a formal tradition. He presents their view in a question, which he answers in unmistakable terms :—

"Theological determinations, ecclesiastical theses, in a word, the whole vast accretion of dogma! That is precisely our real difficulty. And if we excise all that from Christianity, should we not perform a mortal operation upon the religion itself?"

Yes, undoubtedly, I think you would. I think, moreover, you would be a fool for your pains. Nothing is so stupid as an anachronism. Christianity comes before us "rich with the spoils of time." We may take it or leave it. But if we cannot take it as it is, with its doctrines and its traditions, we had better leave it.[1]

While Mr. Lilly's criticism of those who disagree with him is often vigorous and acute, his method of arguing with them on their own principles is, unhappily, not altogether conclusive. He has, indeed, no difficulty in showing the ridiculous side of Atheism as represented in a certain *Freethinker's Catechism*. But it is a curious way of demolishing the views of a writer like the late M. Renan to concede that, of his two reasons for ceasing to believe in Christianity—inability to receive the traditional view of its sacred books, and the conviction that the miracles which they report are impossible—M. Renan was perfectly right in the one, and in the other was merely refusing credit to what cannot be accepted as a credential of Christianity. To maintain that if Christianity depended upon the traditional thesis as to the documents composing the Bible, Christianity would be doomed,[2] and that

[1] *Op. cit.* p. 310. [2] P. 106.

miracles are no special proof, is in these days not considered unreasonable; but assuredly the admission comes strangely from any one who demands our belief in a revelation. Yet we find Mr. Lilly admitting that "phenomena, apparently miraculous, are not the monopoly of any particular religious system," and that "thaumaturgy in itself possesses no moral value."[1] Nor, so far as I can perceive, is there any essential disagreement between the two writers in their use of the word "miracle." To M. Renan a miracle was simply that which has not been explained. To Mr. Lilly it is "an event with the laws of whose working we are, and ever must remain, unacquainted."[2] The only difference apparent here is that on the question whether or not certain laws will ever be discovered, Mr. Lilly commits himself to a piece of dogmatism from which M. Renan refrained. In the etymological meaning of the word "miracle," as an event exciting wonder because the conditions of its appearance are not understood, the disputants seem to agree. But in its theological meaning, as an event ouside the complex system of causally determined relations which we call Nature, Mr. Lilly is obviously in no agreement with himself when he talks of "the laws" of its working. If an event happens according to laws, it is not a miracle.

There are many natural phenomena—for example, the facts of variation—with the laws of whose

[1] P. 113.   [2] P. 115.

working we are, and perhaps may always remain, unacquainted. That is hardly a reason for calling them "supernatural." When Mr. Lilly, after giving us his definition of a miracle, describes it as "a supernatural fact," he fails to discern that the use of the word "supernatural" either begs the whole question or is self-contradictory. Further, he makes what to any one acquainted with his opponent's writings must seem the unaccountable statement that, in denying the possibility of a supernatural event, M. Renan was denying the existence of a spiritual principle in man and in nature. But he himself provides the reader with a refutation of this statement. He asserts that "the direct revelation of the personal God is that which is made to the personality of man"; and as an illustration of what he means he quotes a passage from Seneca and another from M. Renan's *Nouvelles Études d'Histoire religieuse*, containing the following declaration:—" So long as there is in the human heart one fibre to vibrate to the sound of what is true, pure, and honest, so long as the instinctively pure soul prefers purity to life . . . so long will God live in us. *Est Deus in nobis.*" It is difficult to understand why Mr. Lilly should quote this passage in this connection, unless he supposes M. Renan to have sincerely believed in the existence of that very spiritual principle which he elsewhere asserts that M. Renan denied.

Nor in battling with Mr. Herbert Spencer does

our critic emerge from the conflict without inflicting
sundry wounds upon himself. That the metaphysical theories of the author of *The Synthetic
Philosophy* are not unimpeachable was discovered
many years ago, and was made especially clear by
Green in his earlier critical essays. Mr. Lilly
now restates with considerable force the objections
that may be taken to these theories, but in driving
the objections home he uses weapons which sometimes tell equally against his own position. He
also falls into strange discrepancies. For example,
in speaking of the Infinite, he denies that any
analysis can reach it; "for to analyse the Infinite
is a contradiction in terms." Still that does
not prevent him from making the following assertion :—

> So much, it seems to me, we *know* concerning the Ultimate
> Reality. . . . I say that Reality is manifested to our consciousness as the Original of the law physical, which rules in the
> phenomenal world, and of the law moral written on the fleshly
> tables of the heart ; as the Supreme Good, in whom all ideas are
> realised ; as the First Cause and Final End of the Universe,
> where all is causation and finality; as the Self-Existent and
> therefore a Person, or rather let us say, with the MundakaUpanishad, "the Person," from whom all personality is an
> effluence.[1]

But as if this were too large an assertion—and for
my part I find a difficulty in conceiving of any that
could well be larger—Mr. Lilly lays down that "all
our words, essentially phenomenal and relative, are

[1]. P. 243.

but sensuous symbols of the great Noumenal Fact, concealing what they express."

That a Roman Catholic writer should speak favourably of mysticism is only to be expected, and accordingly we find it described as the proper complement of a theistic theory, and as pointing the way from phenomena to something behind them. Whether mysticism properly understood possesses any value or is of no value at all, is a question that admits of serious treatment; but the question is one upon which Mr. Lilly has apparently not yet made up his mind, for he advocates the claims of this intellectual and emotional temper with a curious contrariety of assertion. Mysticism, he says, is based on "the indubitable fact that the spirit of man comes into contact with a Higher Spirit, whose manifestations carry with them their own proof." Again, the Infinite and Eternal is said to be no mere article of belief, but an experience.[1] Yet we are also confronted with the statement that mysticism without dogma is apt to issue in "Nihilistic Pessimism." The theologians, says Mr. Lilly, allow that there may be sound sense in mystical speculations, "so long as the Arachne clue of authoritative dogma is held fast in the labyrinth. Once lose it, and you will be compelled to assert either that God is unknowable, or that the inmost essence of the Divinity is the clean opposite of what Christianity declares it to

[1] P. 256.

be." Mysticism, then, according to this statement, has an intrinsic lack of value. As for the results of the mystical temper, we may gather what they are from a candid opinion expressed in regard to Mr. Spencer for his inconsistency in talking of an "inscrutable" Power "manifested" through consciousness: "If Mr. Spencer were talking mysticism, this might hold. But he supposes himself to be talking science."[1] Mr. Spencer's phrase may, indeed, be self-contradictory, but Mr. Lilly has hardly put himself in a position to complain. Nor, in spite of the favour with which he speaks of mysticism, can I discover anything in his treatment of it which lends support to theistic belief.

But the most surprising contradiction of all is yet to be noted. "There is," says Mr. Lilly, "only one Truth, and there is only one way of discerning what is true."[2] Now, as we have seen, the whole tenor of his elaborate argument is to show that those who decline to accept Christianity, or what is vital and essential to it, namely, its dogmas, ignore the teachings of reason, and are sunk in a quagmire of philosophical error. But, if that be so, why, we may ask, should anyone take such a vast amount of trouble for an end that, even if attained, is admitted to be of no practical use? At the close of his argument Mr. Lilly maintains that the Christian evidences "are not of so imperative a character as to impose themselves

[1] P. 150.   [2] P. 3.

... upon reluctant wills. ... If the evidences of Christianity were of such a character that no honest or educated man could possibly reject them without intellectual folly, whatever his moral condition or history might be, the Christian belief would be, like a university degree, a certificate of a certain sort of mental capacity." Let us grant that, but then what becomes of the *argumentum ad hominem?* What becomes of dogma as the essential element in Christianity? Where is the use of psychological demonstration if not to force belief on those cultivated and virtuous men and women beyond the pale? We shall do well to remember that even those beyond the pale may equally, with the dogmatic theologian, be credited with a moral attitude. They may be morally incapable of saying that they know, in mystical or any other fashion, that which in reality they do not know.

One passage alone in *The Great Enigma* would serve to show the instability of the author's theological equilibrium and the strange character of the argument by which he demands submission to the teaching of the Church. In criticising Mr. Spencer he observes that the sole ground on which that philosopher calls upon us to receive a certain doctrine, "under pain, as it were, of intellectual reprobation, is that his philosophy cannot get on without it. That is true enough. But it is hardly a sufficient argument why we should subordinate reason to faith, and accept descriptions as though they were explanations." Nevertheless we are called upon to accept many of Mr. Lilly's doctrines on the ultimate ground that his theology cannot get on without them. "The only logical alternative," he declares, "is to deny the validity of intellect altogether."[1] Yet is it not the fundamental argument of the Roman Church to deny the sufficiency of human reason on all questions of theology, philosophy, and morality?

II

If any doubts remain as to what Mr. Lilly may mean by Christianity, they are effectually dispelled by a later work, in which he professes to discuss the claims of that religion. Its claims, he says, may be reduced to two :—

> First, as a religion, Christianity claims to be the sole and sufficient oracle of divine truth, superseding all other modes of faith, a system of moral discipline for mankind, transforming every human relation by its remedies for sin and its incentives to goodness: the guardian of that tree of life whose leaves are for the healing of the nations. This is what Hume, in a well-known passage, called "the intolerance of Christianity, by which it refused alliance with other religions and insisted on reigning alone or not at all." Secondly, Christianity is not merely an idea; it is also a phenomenon: it is not only a theology; it is also a community. It is a Church, as well as a religion; and as a Church it claims to be a universal spiritual empire. It takes man as he is, a member of a family, a member of a civil corporation, a member of the human race, and it makes him a member of an

---

[1] P. 243.

ecclesiastical society, a character which affects him in all his other capacities.[1]

Their advocate, however, does not devote much attention to the former of these claims, except in a brief discussion of the rival pretensions advanced by Buddhism and by Islam. As we proceed, it drops into the background, and what Christianity requires men to believe comes in effect to mean what Catholicism as a polity requires them to believe.

Now the two "claims" here ascribed to Christianity are two distinct doctrines, of which the first alone recommends itself to the great bulk of sensible Englishmen. To them presumably the defence is addressed. Sensible men will remember, however, that in all argument some undue advantage is apt to be gained where a term is used in one sense by the advocate and understood in another by his audience. Unconsciously he is led to confuse the issue which he desires to place before them, by using the term sometimes in one and sometimes in the other of the senses in which he understands it, just as the exigencies of his argument require. And when, as in the present case, he has a large fund of historical and literary illustration to draw upon, the confusion is not diminished. His argument, amply clothed with illustration, comes to this: that the Catholic Church is an institution divinely ordained for the purpose of restoring "the

[1] *The Claims of Christianity.* By W. S. Lilly, p. 2.

human race to that unity which sin and its consequences have broken"; of organising "a universal spiritual empire"; and of establishing, in the Papacy, a supreme mundane authority for "vindicating the rights of conscience, the prerogatives of the spiritual order, the immunities of the city of God." This Church, as a polity, has been, he says, and still is, of paramount importance to mankind; and the validity of its claim as a polity is that which he is chiefly concerned to defend.

The appeal is to history; but what has history to say of this claim? The Church has had nearly nineteen centuries in which to establish that universal spiritual empire which its advocate asserts to be its destiny, and no such empire has yet been established. Nay, when he attempts to estimate the work of the Church during the time when it wielded the greatest and widest power; when it came nearest to the attainment of empire; when the Church was co-extensive with Christendom and nearly co-extensive with Western civilisation, namely, in the Middle Ages, he is compelled to admit—and his frankness is praiseworthy —that the men of mediæval times, who "breathed an atmosphere of faith," also "perpetrated an enormous amount of wickedness." Yet in the Middle Ages the Church, as a polity, was undoubtedly most prosperous. If there is any sign that this polity was of human and not of divine ordination, we might surely find the sign in the fact that it did not know how to meet prosperity; that when it was most prosperous as a Church it was most corrupt as a religion. We may admit, with Mr. Lilly, that the Pope in those ages of faith exercised legislative and judicial functions of the highest importance, tempered a *régime* of violence with ideas of reciprocal duty, and above all promoted sentiments of loyalty; but that is no more than saying that the Church as a polity was successful when it was kept in prosperity by the interaction of mutual jealousy in other polities. When its work was done, it was overtaken by the fate of all human institutions. What happened to the Papacy we know. The see was removed from Rome to Avignon. Its possession became a subject of bitter rivalries. Finally, over a great part of Christendom its yoke was cast off. Moreover, in the convulsions which followed, the polity was very glad to avail itself of the secular arm whenever the secular arm was stretched out to relieve it. Mr. Lilly, in describing this step as "a monstrous blunder," refers more particularly to the establishment of the Inquisition, and he makes some admirable remarks on "the inexpediency, in the long-run, of attempting to repress by penal legislation religious beliefs and practices, except such as are manifestly subversive of civilised society." Yet he refers with satisfaction to the success which attended the Catholic cause, although brought about by these very means. The Church, indeed, warned by the

Protestant Reformation, began to put its house in order and to suppress its scandals; but it employed sheer force to recover the ground that had been lost. We may maintain, if we choose, that the Council of Trent bore much salutary fruit in vindicating the constitution of the Church and the prerogatives of the Papacy; yet so far was the Church even then from vindicating "the rights of conscience"—a work which Mr. Lilly claims for it—that it persecuted Galileo for following his conscience in a matter of science; it burnt Bruno just as a century before it had burnt Savonarola; and it regained its sway in France and the Low Countries by methods which Catholic apologists usually omit to mention.

But Mr. Lilly is acute enough to see and frank enough to confess that the Papacy will never again attain the same kind of empire which it wielded before the Reformation. He considers, however, that there are reasons for believing that a spiritual empire will take the place of temporal sovereignty. The Church can no longer look to the civil power to execute its decrees; it will look to public opinion, to the public conscience. We are presented with a fanciful picture of the Pope as the spiritual teacher of the New Age.

> I see no prospect that the Catholic Church will again hold the position in Europe which she held in the Middle Ages: that the Pope will once more occupy the great international office assigned him in the canon law. But it is well conceivable that in the New Age, which is even now upon us, the Pontiff's moral

influence will be of unparalleled greatness, as from his seat by the tomb of the Apostles he surveys his ecumenical charge, and

> Listening to the inner flow of things
> Speaks to the age out of eternity:

reproving the world of sin, of righteousness, and of judgment: maintaining the divine testimonies before kings and democracies: upholding the rights of conscience and of the moral law, amid the social tyrannies, the national jealousies, the political animosities, which will doubtless be the staple of future history, as they are of past.[1]

This is, indeed, a burst of enthusiasm. There follows, however, the inevitable reaction of despair. For the writer no sooner gives way to his feelings than he recognises, with obvious reluctance, that the intellectual conditions of the New Age and the problems which the New Age raises are not favourable as yet to the realisation of his hopes. He admits that the great masters of modern literature, from Goethe until now — and who are our spiritual teachers if not they?—are, on the whole, "alien from Catholicism, if not opposed to it." Who of us can doubt that the great masters are likely to remain alien from Catholicism, as the word has hitherto been understood?

The kind of moral influence which this polity will probably exercise in the future can be estimated, if at all, only by the part which it has played in the past. We have no other standard; and while any one is free to conceive that the Church is still destined to establish a universal

---

[1] *Op. cit.* p. 242.

spiritual empire, any one else may with equal freedom conceive that, as in the past, so in the future, it will find itself compelled to take sides in the affairs of the world, and, as heretofore, to become entangled in "the social tyrannies, the national jealousies, the political animosities," from which we can scarcely hope to emerge. And if the Church is henceforth to pose as the vindicator of the rights of conscience, that must be by adopting methods other than those which have characterised it in the past. Yet its advocate in these days is so courageous as to maintain that at the time of the Reformation the Church vindicated those rights ; that the practical outcome of the Reformation was to establish "a secular despotism," which obliterated "the belief that Christian men live under another and a higher law than the law of the State."

What, then, of Luther ? Mr. Lilly confesses that, quite apart from Luther's opinions and works, he does not like him. He dislikes "his arrogance and self-sufficiency ; his ignorance and coarseness ; his violent imagination and bellicose temperament ; and the curious mixture of mysticism and materialism which is ever cropping up in him."

No one, I think, can seriously doubt that dislike of the Reformer couched in terms like these proceeds from a total misconception of the nature of his work. If Luther did anything at all, surely he vindicated "the rights of the religious conscience," which had been outraged by abuses in the Church ; and he did so because he held firmly to the belief that Christian men live under another and a higher law than the law which the Church was then applying. Nay, I venture to affirm that any description of the Church as vindicating the rights of conscience against Luther is a palpable absurdity. Nor is this the only instance in which Mr. Lilly misinterprets the elementary facts of the Reformation. If further example be needed, he denies the accuracy of a statement of Döllinger's, that the separation resulted not so much from the abuses in the Church as for the sake of doctrine. Plainly, what Döllinger meant is perfectly true; namely, that while the abuses were the obvious cause of the revolt, it was on questions of doctrine that Protestantism took its stand.

III

Submission to the authority of the Church in matters of belief is defended by another Roman Catholic Englishman of our day, on somewhat different grounds, and with the use of arguments that do not altogether tally with those of which we have just taken stock. I refer to Mr. Wilfrid Ward and a volume of essays to which he gave the title *Witnesses to the Unseen*. In some respects they form, I think, a valuable contribution to the current literature of theological controversy; for whether or not we agree with the doctrines which they expound, it is perhaps well to have those doctrines stated with as much precision as is consistent with their nature, and with as much skill and learning as can be supplied by a writer who has spared no pains to present them from his own point of view. The essayist is one of the ablest exponents of what may be called the higher Catholicism. Of these apologists I trust that I may say, without doing violence to truth, or without making any assertion which they would be disposed to repel, that while they are familiar with the resources of theological and philosophical argument, and use them with considerable skill, they also know how to make the most of the advantages arising from vague and elastic elements in the Catholic creed. In other words, they appear to be perfectly alive to the nature and effect of the progress which physical science and historical criticism are making, and the further progress which they are likely to make, in undermining the old Catholic position; but they are beset by no fears; for they are also well acquainted with the convenient constitution of a Church which finds the means of adapting its creed to fresh requirements whenever such a course is indispensable to its existence.

In this connection the essay in which Mr. Ward discusses the effect of "New Wine in Old Bottles" is one of the most instructive; for while he there reviews some attempts which have recently been made to find a *modus vivendi* between the Christian faith and the conclusions of science—while he leads us to suppose that those attempts must of necessity end in the bottles being broken and the wine spilled—he maintains at the same time that the Catholic Church can and does put whatever is good in the new wine into the old bottles without any disastrous consequences. The method is simple. The Church waits until the wine has proved its character. If it keeps well; if the conclusions of science and of history are firmly established, it uses them in its own service; for, says Mr. Ward with some courage, "the discoveries of science are among the acknowledged *criteria* used by the Church in the explanation of Scripture."[1] He quotes with manifest approval a passage from an address given by Monsignor d'Hulst to an International Scientific Congress of Catholics at Paris, in which that eminent Catholic defended a dilatory attitude on the part of the Church, and pointed out to his hearers that so long as they showed a common docility to the Church, they were not forbidden to hold their own views on questions of science or criticism on which it had hitherto made no definite pronouncement. Mr. Ward goes further, as the following declaration will show :—

> But this is not all. While individual Catholics often have what may be called a certain provisional power of reconsideration where the Church has not decided authoritatively, we may also see in the Church a power of assimilation and of ultimate consolidation of her teaching in its relations to assured scientific

[1] *Witnesses to the Unseen*, p. 96.

advance, or well-examined and tenable hypothesis. While her caution protects her against those whims of the *Zeitgeist* which prematurely claim the title of discoveries, the activity of her life enables her *in the end* to find a *modus vivendi* with what is really valuable in intellectual movements or really true in scientific achievement. This is a special prerogative of a living authoritative tribunal which, from the nature of the case, cannot be clearly asserted by any ruling power whose nature is documentary. And the Church has on occasion exhibited the principle of progressive assimilation in a marked manner.[1]

A very slight knowledge of history suffices to show that the Church has not always treated scientific novelties with this irreproachable prudence. Indeed, there are not a few who maintain that it is only the existence of a large body of educated opinion which prevents the Church from now acting towards the pioneers of science as it acted in the Middle Ages. The explanation which is given of this ugly difficulty is more ingenious than convincing. We are told that in those days "there was probably less need for toleration for the sake of individual consciences, as scientific discovery had not yet got so firm a foothold as to be in many cases a living source of difficulty." To admit a startling scientific novelty would then, it seems, have endangered the Christian conscience; to yield to a new discovery would have shaken dogmatic beliefs in the minds of persons unable to separate the traditional interpretation of a dogma from its essence. But now the Church takes an exactly

[1] P. 83.

opposite course, because "the over-subtle mind of the present day, readily grasping the real weight of evidence for a new scientific discovery, more readily than formerly distinguishing between the essence and the traditional interpretation of dogmatic belief, has more to fear from the temporary denial of what may prove true, and less to fear from the readjustment of explanations of dogma." The conclusion which the plain man will draw from this ecclesiastical opportunism is not, I imagine, far to seek. He will judge, and, I think, rightly judge, that in regard to science and history— that is, in regard to organised knowledge in large and important branches of human inquiry —the Catholic Church is not in the least concerned to remove old error; nay, that it has a definite motive for preferring old error, if it leaves religious belief undisturbed. I will even go so far as to say that he would scarcely be wrong were he to entertain the belief that this indifference, or rather this opposition, to new truth in some branches of knowledge which the Church admittedly presses into its own service at her own convenience, argues ill for any strict regard for truth in the performance of what has been called its primary duty, that of protecting religious belief in the mass of Christians.

Mr. Ward summarises his position in a few observations on the extent to which contemporary opinion ought to influence private judgment; in a word, on the respect due to the *Zeitgeist*. He finds it a hopeful sign of the present age that, with us at least, contemporary opinion in some degree recognises its own want of accuracy and finality; and clearly, if this be so, the *Zeitgeist* is doing well. I fancy, however, that we shall do ill to presume that the world is on that account about to return to Catholicism.

But, as every one knows, the Catholic Church is as little disposed in these days to exalt reason at the expense of faith as it was in the days of Abelard. In regard to the question which, according to its disciple, the Church has now to solve, faith and not reason will, of course, determine the solution of it. To what extent—so runs the question—ought belief in Christian dogma to be affected by the results of modern science and historical research? This fundamental problem is attacked in *The Wish to Believe*, a series of three dialogues, in which Mr. Ward endeavours to come to close quarters with the real difficulty of his position. There, as elsewhere, he attempts a practical application of the doctrine involved in Newman's theory of an illative sense; the theory, that is to say, that we possess a faculty by which we draw, and are entitled to draw, inferences without any conscious logical process. His object is to show that when, for instance, two men of equal ability view the same evidence for the Christian dogmas, one in a spirit of strict impartiality and the other with a fervent desire to find them true, this wish to believe does not, in the latter case, invalidate the verdict.

In these dialogues the author entertains his readers with a display of intellectual fencing which is not, perhaps, very common in the communion to which he belongs. His main contention is that there is one set of principles for estimating the effect of historical evidence, and another for estimating the effect of religious evidence; and that in the appreciation of religious evidence it makes a radical difference whether or not the investigator intensely wishes that one interpretation should prove true rather than another. A man, he declares, who looks at evidence with equal readiness to draw one conclusion or another, according to the weight of it, is without the true motive power for critical inquiry. We may grant that; but we must still quarrel with the assumption which is maintained throughout that the only interpretation of the evidence which a man thoroughly in earnest will desire to see proved is the Catholic interpretation. The first essential of the *religious* attitude of mind is characterised as "a deep sense of the importance of the knowledge and of the bearing of the fact to be known upon one's self. This immediately issues in a passion for true knowledge based on this sense, and thus passion is enlisted on the side of reason." Even if this be so, we are not entitled to infer that the truth of Catholicism is the only result which a man could ardently desire to attain. A passionate wish to prove the validity, let us say, of a theism like Dr. Martineau's, or an agnosticism like Mr. Huxley's, would make an investigator equally keen in appreciating all the evidence, and equally sensitive to all the clues, that lead to theism or agnosticism; and we can hardly deny that we have theists and agnostics who are passionate in this sense. Mr. Ward, I venture to suggest, does not adequately distinguish between the desire to find some explanation of the facts of life and consciousness, as a refuge from complete scepticism, and the wish that some particular explanation should prove true. Nor can I describe it as other than a mere begging of the question to suppose that the desire for knowledge and the desire to believe must necessarily be confined to the inquirer who finds his theories stilled by Catholicism, or to lay down at the outset that the only or the best explanation of the facts is that which he earnestly wishes to establish.

CHAPTER VIII

THE WITNESS OF HISTORY

I

ONE or two arguments, drawn from certain aspects of the development of thought, remain to be noticed. They have been described, in language that may perhaps be held to assume more than can be proved, as the witness of history. We are sometimes told that the general history of mankind itself discloses the existence of a God; that the fates of individuals and of nations, and the destinies which consciously or unconsciously they have fulfilled, afford a proof stronger than can be derived from merely theoretical reasoning. Others, again, urge that so far from supplying any such proof, the spectacle of the world, as it is and as it has been, gives abundant warrant for doubt and denial. On this vast question whether the course of secular history offers any support to theistic belief, I do not, however, propose to touch. It has often been discussed, although never, I imagine, with any satisfactory result; and it involves a still vaster question, namely, whether any regular development, not alone in religion or morality, but in any other of the great features of individual or social life, has governed human history at all. I need scarcely remind the reader that here the most diverse opinions are possible. He may hold with the extreme view adopted on one side by Hegel, that history is the progressive self-realisation of a Universal Spirit in accordance with a general law; or, flying to the other extreme with Schopenhauer, he may believe that the past exhibits nothing but a constant repetition of the same crimes and rascalities in combinations that do, indeed, vary, but display no more development than the successive shapes taken by the pieces of glass in a kaleidoscope.

The arguments which appear to me to call for some few observations are based, not on any order of events, but solely on the course of philosophical speculation. They are suggested by the perusal of a recent work, entitled *The History of Intellectual Development*, by Mr. Beattie Crozier. From what has already been published of this undertaking, I gather that its purpose is not merely to record the history of thought. It is also to explain that history. It is to trace a line, or law, or principle, in some of the forms which thought has assumed, either as a whole or in particular stages. Mr. Crozier appears to believe that by careful study some such law or principle can be discovered; nay, more, that the law can be grasped so clearly that the student may lay it down at the outset, and then proceed to show that it is scientifically demonstrated by the actual course of intellectual inquiry.

Whether and in what sense the design is practicable will be considered hereafter; but I may say at once that in pursuance of it no attempt is made to fulfil the strict letter of the title. To embark upon a complete survey of the whole thought of the world, wherever or on whatever men may have exercised their minds, and to try to trace a development, would plainly be a hopeless enterprise. The survey is practically restricted to Europe. Although Hindoo thought is examined at some length, the examination seems to be conducted chiefly with the object of deciding whether Eastern speculation is likely to have any very real or profound influence on Western ideas. Further, by *thought* is meant religion, philosophy, and physical science only, in spite of the very obvious fact that art is a channel and expression of thought as important and significant as any of the three. Æschylus has certainly as much claim to a place in the history of thought as Thales or Pythagoras; and in later times no such history could be adequate which failed to deal with Shakespeare. Possibly it is the case that art does not readily lend itself to the illustration of any law of intellectual development; but that, I apprehend, is so much the worse for any attempt to trace that law.

The first question which must confront any careful student has to do with the materials for such a history as is here proposed. Have we a sufficient number of facts bearing on that history to justify our attempt to reduce them to scientific laws, or to prove the truth of those laws when they have been enunciated? The most competent authorities, we are told, will answer in the affirmative. Whether or not such answer be positive and final, certain it is that we have more and better materials at our command now than were possessed by any of those who have previously undertaken a similar or analogous task. Especially in Hindoo thought and in the doctrine and practice of the early Christians much has recently been laid bare that is of prime importance for any such inquiry. So large a survey as may be obtained at present would have been quite impossible even in the middle of the nineteenth century, to say nothing of the beginning. Nor is this the only advantage which an author now enjoys over such writers as Hegel, Buckle, and Comte. He can also profit by their treatment of the facts that were within their reach. He can take warning by their mistakes and shortcomings.

What these were, if the writers be regarded from the point of view which he himself adopts, Mr. Crozier endeavours to show. Hegel, he says, had comparatively so few materials that he was obliged to content himself with the enunciation of a single general law, true enough for intelligence in the abstract, but too wide to be of any value in the particular divisions and periods into which thought has actually fallen. Comte may have accurately described the chief stages of speculation as theological, metaphysical, and positive; but while he could thus suggest how the social and moral phenomena of those stages were to be explained, his law also was not of a kind to determine their inner connection. As for Buckle, he only adopted Comte's classification under other names: he called the theological and metaphysical stages, in their intellectual aspects, the deductive method of inquiry, and the positive or scientific, the inductive; and he did no more than offer a piece of special pleading in favour of science. Nor can we doubt that Mr. Herbert Spencer's Law of Evolution, or of endless differentiation from the vague and indeterminate to the complex and involved, although possibly applicable to the universe as a whole, is barren and useless when offered as a solution of the special problems of intellectual development.

Mr. Crozier reviews the efforts of these writers in order to illustrate the nature and scope of his own. He is not concerned, like Mr. Spencer, in showing how germs, whether of organs or of intelligence, unfold themselves in endless differentiations. His purpose is to trace the development of lower ideas into higher in the thought of civilised nations. It is not so much with the mere succession of intellectual theories that he has to do as with the increasing degree in which they accord with the needs of human nature, and with their influence on ethical codes and on ideals of life. If he proposes to exhibit what he calls "the curve of evolution" in special systems, be they only philosophies or religions as well, it is to indicate their effect in expanding and ennobling the human spirit.

The whole undertaking has, I venture to think, a distinct value apart from the measure of success which may attend its special purpose. Mr. Crozier is possessed of considerable insight into the true bearing of great intellectual systems, and of their relation one to another; he marshals his facts with skill, and expresses them in language that is always precise and often eloquent. Although what he has produced is not in the ordinary sense a history of philosophy, it is far more valuable, let alone more interesting, than many works that pass by that name. The conceptions formed of the intellectual movements passed in review are many of them to be found elsewhere; but what is unique in the treatment is the clearness with which their connection is described. Here, of course, their connection is the matter with which the historian is especially concerned, because he is desirous of showing that they are stages in one great development. This leads him to emphasise features of systems which have not, I think, previously been emphasised. That he has studied his authorities with care and intelligence, and that he has made the best use of them, may be inferred from the comprehensive character of his survey, and the ease and simplicity with which he traces the essential features of a theory or sums up the bearings of a question.

In order that the reader may have some opportunity of testing for himself the validity of the general argument which is here advanced, I propose very briefly to sketch the development of thought according to the mode in which Mr. Crozier presents it. The views, he tells us, which men entertain of the world will depend on the nature of the causes by which they conceive its phenomena to be produced. These causes he roughly classifies as religious, metaphysical, and scientific, or, more accurately, as personal wills, abstract essences, and physical antecedents. In his survey of the evolution of Greek thought he likens that thought to a boat upon a vast stream. The boat is philosophy, and the banks of the stream are religion and science. The philosophers revolted against the popular polytheism, and started from the scientific shore. But as one physical antecedent after another failed them, they were compelled in their own despite to make for the region of wills, to move farther and farther away from the point at which they started, until their course finally landed them on the shores of Christianity. The tendencies represented, say by Democritus, equally with those which found their expression in Socrates, were, says our guide, certain to fail; the one because they had none of the unifying energy of religion, the other because they were not susceptible of scientific proof. Plato's system, built up out of the elements reached by previous philosophers, viz. the good, ideas, number, and matter or the ἄπειρον, he maintains to have been *statically* complete, but to have failed as an explanation of the world because it lacked a dynamical or evolutionary principle. This was, if not supplied, at least adumbrated by Aristotle, who conceived that the earth was a potentiality rendered actual by the motion of the æther working upon it. The Stoics attempted to go further still in the direction of a dynamical unity of the world. They paved the way for the Neo-Platonists, who by the theory of emanation contrived to add to the statical perfection of Plato a dynamical principle equally perfect. The step from the abstract essences of Neo-Platonism to the personal wills of Christianity was not a great one, and *ex hypothesi crozierana* it was a step which philosophy might naturally have been expected to take.

Before we pass to the development of the theory of a Personal Will reached by Christianity, united with that of a single God for which the way was prepared by Judaism, we are offered a succinct statement of the main conceptions of Hindoo thought. There is considerable force in the suggestion that Hindoo thought can never have any real effect on European religious philosophy because it acknowledges no principle of intelligence in its

Supreme Power or First Cause; and that European philosophy having reached this principle, drawn from what is highest in the human mind, can never go back; but we need not trace the actual steps by which this conclusion is reached. Nor would it be in place here to go over the ground which is traversed in describing the development of Judaism and Christianity, although Mr. Crozier's account of the growth of Monotheism among the people of Israel is remarkable, not only as an excellent summary of the last results of modern scholarship, but also for the skill with which he depicts the operation in Judaism of what he calls the great evolving centres or nuclei of all religions—the Conception of God, the Supernatural Ideal, and the Moral Code. He insists, and rightly insists, on the importance of arriving at a clear notion of what the Jews actually meant by these aspects of their faith, for the simple reason that such knowledge will resolve difficulties in the interpretation of early Christianity which could not otherwise be explained. He argues, that is to say—and this is the very essence of his theory of intellectual development—that if we clearly understand the condition of Jewish thought just before the appearance of Christianity, we shall be able to say what the next stage of it, as represented by Christianity, ought to be; and that of two contradictory interpretations of the original Christian doctrine, that one is most likely to be true which would naturally have developed out of the thought prevailing immediately before it.

Although a large use of this argument may justifiably be made, and is made, on the whole, with success, I cannot but express my own view that in all such accounts of the early growth of Christianity insufficient room is left for the direct personal influence of Christ Himself.

But I do not here propose to examine any of the objections which may be raised on special points in Mr. Crozier's *History*, however numerous or important such objections may be. The only feature of the work that I desire to bring to the reader's notice, as bearing to some extent on the problem discussed in these pages, is the attempt to prove that thought develops according to law; with the admission that, when all is said, there is something in the intellectual products of the world for which no explanation based on purely scientific grounds can adequately account. There are, however, some lines of argument, not unconnected with the main design, to which I may, perhaps, for a moment advert. Any history covering so wide a field must almost of necessity contain many statements which are broadly correct, but will not bear too rigid application to all the facts which they are intended to describe. In the present case an instance of this is supplied by the general contrast indicated between the essential spirit of pagan religion and that of Christianity. The spirit of paganism is summed up in the relationship of master and slave; that of Christianity in the relation of parent and child. While this statement, no doubt, is partly true, it is too concise and absolute. Even when every allowance is made for the fact that the relationship of parent and child in the ancient world had an aspect which was certainly harsh, I fancy that the ancient gods would themselves cry out against the view that the religion which they embodied is to be summed up in the relationship of master and slave. Zeus, at least, might plead that he was commonly invoked as the father of gods and men, and under his Latin name had no other meaning than the sky-father. Again, while the distinction suggested between the indirect method of civilisation in the ancient world and the direct method of later times is a fruitful and luminous idea, it is, perhaps, a little overstated. It has results, too, which are not altogether satisfactory. It compels us to conceive of the co-ordinating Power, or God, as furthering morality by a system of imposture masquerading as supernaturalism. To affirm that Greek philosophy found its logical goal in Christianity is also, I apprehend, too absolute an assertion, although it is made in the same breath with another which is rather more true; namely, that the new principle which was to change the spirit of paganism had to come from without.

II

But this last criticism is, in effect, to raise the whole question to which Mr. Crozier endeavours to supply the answer. Is there any means of showing that thought develops according to law? Can we hope, with any prospect of success, to trace a process of intellectual evolution? With the main contention that, given some general principle, for example, "intelligence," which dominated European thought from the beginnings of Greek philosophy down to the advent of modern science, or the "vital principle" of Indian speculation, or the "physical mechanism" of the modern investigator, this principle will run through the whole gamut of possible modifications in its struggle towards perfect expression—with this contention, I say, no one can have any serious quarrel. Nor is it other than a useful work to describe the development of leading ideas in Greek philosophy, in Judaism, and in Christianity; or to show that the uncertainties attaching to any stage in the history of thought may be reduced, if not finally dispelled, by selecting the position which is most likely to have resulted from the prior conditions.

But assuredly it is a long step from tracing a development already known, and indicating its probability, to the very different process of proving that that development takes place in accordance with any established law. Zeal for the application of a theory of intellectual development may be easily transformed into an excessive confidence in the possibility of prediction, whereby, perhaps, even the legitimate uses of the theory may suffer. There is a certain sagacious maxim bidding us not to prophesy unless we know, and I imagine that what may be described as retrospective prediction is safe only because we have the facts before us. We may agree, indeed, that as between two or more men thought evolves, if by evolution we mean no more than that one of them, by pondering on the views of his predecessor, may succeed in entertaining others of his own, more complicated and more, or possibly less, adapted to the facts of life. We may even be able to trace some order in a given sequence of theories, if the later ones correct the deficiencies of the earlier. But to attempt to define a law or principle of the evolution of theories, and to show that that principle is scientifically demonstrable, is a venture which, at least in our present state of knowledge, has little hope of success. For what can we mean by law or principle in this sense if it is not a method? and where are we to look for the method by which theories evolve? We are familiar with the main factor by the operation of which, on the Darwinian hypothesis, the physical development of the world proceeds. Assuming for the moment that that hypothesis is entirely correct—and it is the only hypothesis now generally accepted—have we any reason to maintain that the life and permanence of theories can be explained on any similar principle? Does the successful theory owe the permanence which it possesses to the fact that its adaptability to its environment has preserved it in the struggle for existence with other theories less favoured? If we could prove that, we should have established a law of intellectual development on those lines of modern evolution which the history of that development professes to follow. But who has proved it? And even were it proved, such an explanation would leave out of account the spasmodic manner in which theories appear, and also the most important, but at the same time the least calculable of all the factors that go to the making of theories, namely, the individuality of the theorist. That one theory is incompetent to explain the facts is not, of course, in itself an argument for the validity of another; but rather than accept the explanation offered, the reader would, I believe, be better advised to entertain a teleological conception as the principle of intellectual development—some such conception as Mr. Crozier, recognising that his theory is inadequate, declares to have been forced upon him by "the spectacle of so many generations of human souls all moving unconsciously towards a predestined end."

Thinkers have not yet solved all the difficulties inherent in the notion of a co-ordinating Power making for a moral end, and shaping the intellectual efforts of the human race so as best to attain it. What these difficulties are, some of the considerations examined in the course of the preceding pages will have told us. Mr. Crozier affirms—and his whole attitude towards the problem is a witness to his sincerity—that he approached his inquiry with a mind free from all religious and philosophical preconceptions; although possibly it may be felt that the notion of thought evolving according to any discoverable scientific law is a preconception of a tolerably large kind. He had not gone far, he says, before he discovered that when all scientific explanations of the phenomena under discussion had been given, there still remained something which they were powerless to explain: something which held the phenomena together, and seemed to force them to a definite and predetermined goal. This unknown Power, he continues, discloses its presence more in religions than in philosophies, constraining men — often against their will and unknown to them—to a state of higher and higher moral or social relation. Were individual men themselves conscious of being means and instruments in the production of this end, their whole activity would be merely that of the human spirit working after its own laws and advancing its own ideals. But history shows us that they are no more conscious of the final result of their efforts than the bees are conscious that in their search for honey they are fertilising the flowers. The assumption, then, is forced upon us that this moral tendency is due to some co-ordinating Power which is not ourselves; and we are thus led to believe in what has been called "a stupendous and over-arching supernaturalism everywhere enfolding and pervading the world and its affairs, and giving scope and exercise to all that is properly religious in thought and feeling."

There is, I think, no serious difficulty in accepting this conclusion, and also at the same time refusing to express adherence to any of the particular religions in which, often mixed with quite alien elements, the conclusion has been embodied. In other words, we may, like our historian, entertain this general belief without laying emphasis on any of the special forms of supernaturalism which have prevailed in the world, or subjecting our treatment of history to any greater disturbance than we should encounter if we recognised an unmeaning Fate to be the inmost principle of all things. To make this assumption frankly, intelligently, and on a large scale, is, in effect, to do no more than what even agnostic philosophers, as we have abundantly discovered, find themselves compelled to do. Like them, we examine the evidence as it is known and at hand, and we find it insufficient to account for the actual result produced. Like them, too, we postulate some additional factor, and describe it as Fate, unknown Power, God, or whatever other term may be in best accord with our inmost convictions.

But so far as the origin and the growth of religion and morality are concerned, I must confess that for my part I fail to perceive any very cogent reason for regarding these features of human life as the exclusive work of some co-ordinating Power which is not ourselves; or why the human spirit alone—little as we understand its nature—should be unable to engender the tendency towards higher moral and social relations. I am not familiar with the precise arguments which forbid us to hold that we may receive some such direction from the individuals who best embody this spirit—those rare personalities which appear from time to time to show mankind of what it is capable. Why, I ask, may we not maintain that religion and morality grow, after the same fashion as art and science, by the intuitions of genius, which, although sometimes pronounced to be supernatural, is the flower of our common humanity?

In a previous page of these Notes I have touched upon the admission, made in our day by an exponent of science, that we owe our ideals of moral grandeur, equally with our ultimate conceptions of science and art, to the insight of gifted individuals; and that both are in the same degree instinctive and innate. Not otherwise, I submit, should we regard religion. To derive it from the human spirit is not to abase it, but to exalt the other possessions which we receive from the same source. Who of us can tell how the interpreter of nature secures us a footing in the regions of the unknown? Who will pretend that he fully understands the mysteries of Art, or has reached the pinnacle where its votary, by a method strange to himself, obtains a vision of ideal truth? Where is the philosopher who will lay bare to our view the secret springs of goodness and justice? To any other origin than that which supplies us, however incomprehensibly, with what we have of Art or Science or Morality, we cannot, surely, with any show of reason, ascribe that complex sphere of thought and feeling where in their highest flights the three are united. In the end, all of them are alike humanly inexplicable; all of them, if we will, are alike divine. It is thus, I am persuaded, that we should accept the witness of history so far as religion is concerned; it is thus that we should revere the teachers who by their genius have attained a loftier view than is granted to common humanity. Then, I believe, and then only, shall we rightly approach our heritage of revelations if we regard them all as reflected from a great Reality, which in our twilight is dimly perceived and, as we look back, is seen to illumine the summits of the past.

Printed by R. & R. CLARK, LIMITED, *Edinburgh.*

In two vols., demy 8vo., cloth, price 24s.

St. Thomas of Canterbury:
HIS DEATH AND MIRACLES.

BY

EDWIN A. ABBOTT, M.A., D.D.,

FORMERLY FELLOW OF ST. JOHN'S COLLEGE, CAMBRIDGE,
AND HULSEAN LECTURER;
AUTHOR OF 'PHILOCHRISTUS,' 'ONESIMUS.'

IN TWO VOLUMES

Illustrated with a Photogravure Frontispiece.

'It is clear that I cannot say much of these six hundred and sixty large pages in the same number of lines. But I would commend them to students of the New Testament, to critics and theologians, as furnishing, with admirable candour, no small addition to their means of following out certain long-debated problems, until they arrive at a solution which shall be true to the evidence.'—*Bookman.*

'A couple of volumes singularly interesting, not only for their naïve human matter and for their important critical implications, but also for the admirably scholarly and sympathetic treatment which he has given them.'—*Academy.*

'Dr. Abbott's book on St. Thomas of Canterbury is one of the most striking contributions, in my belief, to the history of testimony that has ever been made.' —*Inquirer.*

'A thoughtful and eminently scholarly work . . . a work which the student of theology, history, and sociology will regard as one of interest and importance.' —*Scotsman.*

'The critical discernment of Dr. Abbott, the candour and fairness of his criticism, his moderation in tone, and his freedom from partisan prejudice, deserve our warmest praise.'—*Daily News.*

'It is extremely thorough and remarkably accurate; a little hypercritical, no doubt, but very acute and suggestive.'—*Guardian.*

'As to the interest of the story, the scholarly and scientific treatment of his materials, and the great value of the book, no doubt can be entertained.'— *Standard.*

'It should find a place in the library of every clergyman, for it must stimulate inquiry and open out fresh lines of thought, and to any serious student of ecclesiastical history the book will be of special value.'—*Morning Post.*

A. & C. BLACK, SOHO SQUARE, LONDON.

THE APOCALYPSE OF BARUCH.
Translated from the Syriac
By REV. R. H. CHARLES, M.A.
TRINITY COLLEGE, DUBLIN, AND EXETER COLLEGE, DUBLIN.

Crown 8vo., cloth, price 7s. 6d. net.

'Mr. Charles's work will have a hearty welcome from students of Syriac whose interest is linguistic, and from theological students who have learned the value of Jewish and Christian pseudepigraphy; and the educated general reader will find much of high interest in it, regard being had to its date and its theological standpoint.'—*Record.*

'The learned footnotes which accompany the translation throughout will be found most helpful to the reader. Indeed, nothing seems to have been left undone which could make this ancient writing intelligible to the student.'—*Scotsman.*

THE ASSUMPTION OF MOSES.
Translated from the Latin Sixth Century MS., the unemended Text of which is published herewith, together with the Text in its restored and critically emended form.

EDITED, WITH INTRODUCTION, NOTES, AND INDICES.
By REV. R. H. CHARLES, M.A.

Crown 8vo., cloth, price 7s. 6d.

'In this admirable little book the Rev. R. H. Charles has added another to the excellent series of editions by which he has earned the gratitude of all students of early Christian literature.'—*Times.*

'Nothing has been left undone by the author which could contribute to the settling of the text, the elucidation of the general purpose of the book, and the interpretation of particular passages. In short, it is worthy to rank with his edition of the "Apocalypse of Baruch," and higher praise than that could hardly be given.'—*Primitive Methodist Quarterly Review.*

STUDIES IN HEBREW PROPER NAMES.
By G. BUCHANAN GRAY, M.A.,
LECTURER IN HEBREW AND OLD TESTAMENT THEOLOGY IN MANSFIELD COLLEGE;
LATE SENIOR KENNICOTT SCHOLAR IN THE UNIVERSITY OF OXFORD.

Crown 8vo., cloth, price 7s. 6d. net.

'The study of Hebrew proper names, then, with their meaning, their origin, and their classification, cannot be looked upon simply as a dry-as-dust branch of inquiry, but is one full of interest to the Biblical scholar who looks below the surface.'—*Church Quarterly Review.*

'These "Studies" may be warmly commended as a step in the right direction. They bring out into clear relief progress of religious ideas in Israel, and make an important contribution to the criticisms of Old Testament documents.'—C. H. TOY, Harvard University.

'There is not a student of the Old Testament in Hebrew but will find it indispensable.'—*Expository Times.*

A. & C. BLACK, SOHO SQUARE, LONDON.

Demy 8vo., cloth, price 24s.

INTRODUCTION
TO THE
BOOK OF ISAIAH.

WITH AN APPENDIX CONTAINING THE UNDOUBTED PORTIONS OF THE TWO CHIEF PROPHETIC WRITERS IN A TRANSLATION.

BY THE

Rev. T. K. CHEYNE, M.A., D.D.,

ORIEL PROFESSOR OF THE INTERPRETATION OF HOLY SCRIPTURE AT OXFORD, AND FORMERLY FELLOW OF BALLIOL COLLEGE; CANON OF ROCHESTER.

'This elaborate and scholarly work. . . . We must leave to professed scholars the detailed appreciation of Professor Cheyne's work. His own learning and reputation suffice to attest its importance.'—*The Times.*

'This truly great and monumental work.'—*Critical Review.*

'This monument of patient scholarship, wide reading, and indefatigable research.'—*The Speaker.*

In crown 8vo., cloth, gilt top, price 6s.; or in white vellum cloth, extra gilt, gilt top, price 7s. 6d.

PASSAGES OF THE BIBLE,
CHOSEN FOR THEIR LITERARY BEAUTY AND INTEREST.

BY

J. G. FRAZER, M.A.,

FELLOW OF TRINITY COLLEGE, CAMBRIDGE.

'He has given us a fascinating book, the perusal of which cannot fail to invest the Bible, even for many of those who know it best, with a fresh interest and significance.'—*Westminster Gazette.*

'Hardly a verse or a song that rings in anyone's memory but will be found here.'—*Bookman.*

'Mr. Frazer's selections are, as was to be expected, made with care and taste, and he has prefixed to each of them an appropriate heading.'—*Athenæum.*

'The notes are simply admirable.'—*National Observer.*

A. & C. BLACK, SOHO SQUARE, LONDON.

In two vols., demy 8vo., cloth.

NATURALISM AND AGNOSTICISM
THE GIFFORD LECTURES DELIVERED BEFORE THE UNIVERSITY OF ABERDEEN IN THE YEARS 1896—1898.

BY

JAMES WARD, Sc.D., Hon. LL.D. (Edin.),
PROFESSOR OF MORAL PHILOSOPHY AND LOGIC IN THE UNIVERSITY OF CAMBRIDGE.

This work (consisting of five parts) seeks to show that the union of Naturalism and Agnosticism which constitutes 'modern scientific thought,' though it has led to a widespread prejudice against Idealism and so against Theism, has yet really promoted the interest of both. 1. It has brought out the abstract descriptive character of the *Mechanical Theory*, which had been regarded as presenting 'what actually goes on behind what we see and feel.' 2. The futility of attempts, such as that of Mr. Spencer, to deduce the *Evolution* of life, mind, and society from a single mechanical principle is then evident. 3. Further, the *Relation of Body and Mind* has to be treated as a 'correspondence' that is neither causal physically nor casual logically. 4. The perplexities of this *Dualism* lead to a neutral (or agnostic) monism, which—being essentially unstable—must either lapse back into Materialism or advance to Idealism. Reflection upon experience as a whole shows how this Dualism has arisen, and also that it is false. 5. It becomes clear that only in *terms of Mind* can we understand the unity, activity, and regularity that Nature presents.

In one vol., demy 8vo., cloth, price 7s. 6d.

THE QUEST OF FAITH.
BEING NOTES ON THE CURRENT PHILOSOPHY OF RELIGION.

By T. BAILEY SAUNDERS.

In this work the author deals with those theories on the justification of religious belief which have recently found very prominent expression in this country. Nothing is more remarkable in our time than the extent to which the leaders of English opinion, particularly in politics, have discussed the questions which lie at the root of the philosophy of religion. Mr. Bailey Saunders here states and criticises the views of those who make contemporary opinion on this subject. Reviewing the contributions of men like Professor Huxley, Mr. Arthur Balfour, the Duke of Argyll, Mr. Gladstone, and the Roman Catholic writers, he expressly aims at providing the general reader interested in current controversy with an indication of the character and value of their arguments, and an estimate of the general conclusion to which they tend.

In one vol., crown 8vo., cloth, price 1s. 6d. net.

THOUGHTS ON THE PRESENT POSITION
OF
PROTESTANTISM
By Prof. ADOLF HARNACK.
Translated by THOMAS BAILEY SAUNDERS.

This is a version of a recent utterance on the question at issue between the Catholic and the Protestant by the most distinguished German theologian now living. Professor Harnack treats of this question in a brief compass, but with a breadth of view and a vigour of expression which must make what he says interesting to readers of every shade of opinion.

A. & C. BLACK, SOHO SQUARE, LONDON.

Crown 8vo., cloth, price 1s. 6d. net each.

CHRISTIANITY AND HISTORY.

By ADOLF HARNACK.

Translated, with the Author's sanction, by THOMAS BAILEY SAUNDERS, with an Introductory Note.

'It is highly interesting and full of thought. The short introductory note with which Mr. Saunders prefaces it is valuable for its information and excellent in its tone.'—*Athenæum*.

'A singularly able exposition and defence of Christianity, as seen in the newer light, by one of the most learned and acute "evangelical" critics of Germany. The essay is a masterly one.'—*Glasgow Herald*.

'... We hope the lecture will be widely read.'—*Primitive Methodist Quarterly Review*.

'A remarkable paper read to the German Evangelical Union.'—*Scotsman*.

'The lecture itself is weighty in its every word, and should be read and reread by those desiring to have in a nutshell the central positions of modern Christianity.'—*Christian World*.

'We are thankful to Harnack for his splendid vindication of history, and grateful to him for many other things in this lecture.'—*Aberdeen Free Press*.

THE VITALITY OF CHRISTIAN DOGMAS, AND THEIR POWER OF EVOLUTION.

A STUDY IN RELIGIOUS PHILOSOPHY.

By A. SABATIER, D.D.,

DEAN OF THE FACULTY OF PROTESTANT THEOLOGY, PARIS.

Translated by MRS. EMMANUEL CHRISTEN.

With a Preface by the Very Rev. the Hon. W. H. FREMANTLE, D.D., Dean of Ripon.

'Dr. Sabatier has rendered a good and timely service, alike to theology and religion, by discussing, as he does here, the relation in which dogma stands to the reality of religious feeling and experience.'—*Glasgow Herald*.

'This interesting and able volume. We cannot speak too highly of the manner in which Mrs. Christen has translated it. She has rendered into clear and vigorous English not the mere words, but the thoughts and arguments of the original.'—*Pall Mall Gazette*.

'It is really a gem of theological and instructive criticism. The work is worthy the careful attention of all religious teachers.'—*Christian World*.

'It is a powerful and thoughtful study of dogma in the light of modern scientific doctrine.'—*Scotsman*.

'Professor Sabatier has done an excellent service to liberal Christians of all denominations.'—*New Age*.

MONISM; OR, THE CONFESSION OF FAITH OF A MAN OF SCIENCE.

By PROFESSOR ERNST HAECKEL.

Translated from the German by J. D. F. GILCHRIST.

'The Monism, which is the substance of his faith, is thus defined by him: "Our conviction that there lives one spirit in all things, and that the whole cognizable world is constituted, and has been developed, in accordance with one common fundamental law." As the confession of a distinguished man of science, this little work deserves to be read.'—*North British Daily Mail*.

'We may readily admit that Professor Haeckel has stated his case with the clearness and courage which we should expect of him, and that his lecture may be regarded as a fair and authoritative statement of the views now held by a large number of scientifically educated people.'—*Times*.

A. & C. BLACK, SOHO SQUARE, LONDON.

Works by the late W. Robertson Smith, M.A., LL.D.,
PROFESSOR OF ARABIC IN THE UNIVERSITY OF CAMBRIDGE.

Demy 8vo. Price 15s. net.

LECTURES ON THE RELIGION OF THE SEMITES,

THE FUNDAMENTAL INSTITUTIONS.

New Edition. Revised throughout by the Author.

Demy 8vo. Price 10s. 6d.

THE OLD TESTAMENT IN THE JEWISH CHURCH.

A COURSE OF LECTURES ON BIBLICAL CRITICISM.

Second Edition. Revised and much Enlarged.

Post 8vo. Price 10s. 6d.

THE PROPHETS OF ISRAEL

AND THEIR PLACE IN HISTORY

To the Close of the Eighth Century B.C.

Second Edition.

WITH INTRODUCTION AND ADDITIONAL NOTES.

BY

The Rev. T. K. CHEYNE, M.A., D.D.,
ORIEL PROFESSOR OF THE INTERPRETATION OF HOLY SCRIPTURE AT OXFORD,
CANON OF ROCHESTER.

A. & C. BLACK, SOHO SQUARE, LONDON.

In one volume, large crown 8vo., cloth, gilt top, price 7s. 6d.

THE HISTORY OF THE
REFORMATION OF RELIGION
WITHIN THE REALM OF SCOTLAND.

WRITTEN BY
JOHN KNOX.
EDITED FOR POPULAR USE BY
C. J. GUTHRIE, Q.C.

WITH NOTES, SUMMARY, GLOSSARY, INDEX, AND FIFTY-SIX ILLUSTRATIONS.

'The task is one which Carlyle desired to see accomplished nearly thirty years ago, when he wrote in one of the least known of his works: "It is really a loss to English, and even to universal, literature, that Knox's hasty and strangely interesting, impressive, and peculiar book . . . has not been rendered far more extensively legible to serious mankind at large than is hitherto the case." It will be interesting to see if Mr. Guthrie's labour can restore John Knox's "History" to the place of honour it once held, but seems long to have lost, among Scottish classics.'—*Glasgow Herald.*

'Nothing more graphic in incidents and portraiture, or trustworthy in narrative, than this history remains to us of the literature of the period. The book represents an immense amount of labour, and needs only to be casually examined to convince one of the editor's intelligent care in its preparation, and of its present-day value. The foot-notes are invariably fresh and informative.'—*Pray and Trust Magazine.*

Crown 8vo., cloth, price 6s. net.

A SHORT HISTORY
OF
SYRIAC LITERATURE.

BY THE LATE
WILLIAM WRIGHT, LL.D.,
PROFESSOR OF ARABIC IN THE UNIVERSITY OF CAMBRIDGE.

'A masterly account of the literature written in that language. It may safely be said that there is no one in England—or even in Europe—at the present time capable of speaking with anything like his authority in matters appertaining to Syriac literature.'—*Record.*

'A very complete and valuable handbook to this important subject.'—*Pall Mall Gazette.*

'A valuable contribution to an important subject by one well qualified to give the best instruction.'—*Religious Review of Reviews.*

'It is one of those collections of "clotted learning" which are the delight of the scholar, and provoke the respectful admiration of the ordinary reader. Syriac students will be glad to have this handbook in convenient form.'—*British Weekly.*

A. & C. BLACK, SOHO SQUARE, LONDON.

VOL. I. READY IN OCTOBER.
Half-yearly   20s. net

To be Published in Four Quarterly Volumes, Price 16s. each, bound in Cloth.
Size, Super-Royal 8vo., 10 by 7 inches.

For the convenience of Subscribers who wish to bind the work in One Volume when complete, an edition of each of the Quarterly Parts will also be issued on thin paper, in paper boards with leather backs.

ENCYCLOPÆDIA BIBLICA:
A Dictionary of the Bible.

EDITED BY

THE REV. T. K. CHEYNE, M.A., D.D.,

Oriel Professor of the Interpretation of Holy Scripture at Oxford, and formerly Fellow of Balliol College, Canon of Rochester;

AND

J. SUTHERLAND BLACK, M.A., LL.D.,

Assistant Editor of the 'Encyclopædia Britannica.'

THE following are special points that have been kept steadily in view in the preparation of this work:

1. The primary aim has been to supply a much felt want by applying to every detail within the scope of a Bible Dictionary the most exact scientific methods now in use, so as to provide, in dictionary form, the results of a thoroughgoing critical study of the Bible, with a completeness and conciseness that has never yet been attained in any language.

2. The policy adopted is to give a carefully considered account of the subjects dealt with, based on and starting from the latest that has been written on the subject by the leading scholars, rather than to attempt to calculate the average opinion in the world of Biblical studies.

3. Generally speaking, the subject-matter of the 'Encyclopædia Biblica' is that of Bible dictionaries in general. Some large important headings will, however, be found here for the first time, and archæological facts have been treated with greater fulness than has been usual in works of this class. By a careful system of cross-references to general articles, and by the admission of only such parts of a subject as directly affect Biblical questions, it has been found possible to treat many headings with greater brevity than in previous works in the same field. For facility of reference all the larger articles have been divided into numbered sections, with sub-headings printed in clear type.

4. Great pains have been taken and much thought has been expended with the view of avoiding repetitions, and attaining the greatest possible condensation, especially in minor matters, so as to secure adequate treatment of all questions of primary importance.

5. The work has, on the whole, proceeded simultaneously throughout the alphabet, so that all the articles, from the largest to the very smallest, might be collated with each other in as far as they are mutually dependent or illustrative; the results of this collation being given in very full references to the numerical section of the cognate article.

6. By delaying the stereotyping to the very last, it has been possible to work the results of new discoveries or fresh discussions, as they appear from month to month, into the whole mass of articles.

A. & C. BLACK, SOHO SQUARE, LONDON.

www.ingramcontent.com/pod-product-compliance
Lightning Source LLC
Chambersburg PA
CBHW020921230426
43666CB00008B/1529